BUY BACK
YOUR TIME

BUY
BACK
YOUR
TIME

Get Unstuck, Reclaim Your Freedom, and Build Your Empire

DAN MARTELL

PORTFOLIO / PENGUIN

PORTFOLIO / PENGUIN
An imprint of Penguin Random House LLC
penguinrandomhouse.com

Most Portfolio books are available at a discount when purchased in
quantity for sales promotions or corporate use. Special editions, which
include personalized covers, excerpts, and corporate imprints,
can be created when purchased in large quantities. For more information,
please call (212) 572-2232 or e-mail specialmarkets@penguinrandomhouse.com.
Your local bookstore can also assist with discounted bulk purchases using the
Penguin Random House corporate Business-to-Business program. For assistance
in locating a participating retailer, e-mail B2B@penguinrandomhouse.com.

Diagrams designed by Rich Gould.

LIBRARY OF CONGRESS CATALOGING-IN-PUBLICATION DATA
Names: Martell, Dan (Business consultant), author.
Title: Buy back your time : get unstuck, reclaim your freedom,
and build your empire / Dan Martell.
Description: New York : Portfolio/Penguin, [2023] |
Includes bibliographical references and index.
Identifiers: LCCN 2022029414 (print) | LCCN 2022029415 (ebook) |
ISBN 9780593422977 (hardcover) | ISBN 9780593422984 (ebook)
Subjects: LCSH: Time management. | Entrepreneurship. | Success in business.
Classification: LCC HD69.T54 M3794 2023 (print) | LCC HD69.T54 (ebook) |
DDC 650.1/1—dc23/eng/20220624
LC record available at https://lccn.loc.gov/2022029414
LC ebook record available at https://lccn.loc.gov/2022029415

Printed in the United States of America
12th Printing

BOOK DESIGN BY TANYA MAIBORODA

Names and identifying characteristics have been changed
to protect the privacy of the individuals involved.

To Renée, Max, and Noah, you are my everything.

Contents

How Business Saved My Life (Then Almost Ruined It)

I STARED AT THE GUN in my duffel bag.

If I just point it at these cops, they'll end my miserable life for me.

Wiping the sweat from my eyes, I peered into the rearview mirror. Two armed police officers were racing toward my car. I'd just led them on a high-speed chase and crashed into the side of a house. They'd finally caught up and had every reason to fire on sight. It was game over.

Hopelessness flooded me. Memories of a lifetime of troubled antics. Shoplifting in grade school. Stints in group homes in middle school. Getting booted from high school.

When my mom found drugs, money, and stolen guns at our house, she'd finally had enough and called the cops. But my brother Pierre tipped me off, so instead of waiting around to get arrested, I took the $63 he offered and went on the run, hiding in hunting camps and crashing on friends' couches. Finally, after weeks of trying to stay one step ahead of the police, I decided to leave my small Canadian town of Moncton, New Brunswick, and head to Montreal, where my uncle lived.

I stole a car and left town—but I didn't get far. I was on the road only a short time when I hit a random roadblock. Feeding the cops a bogus story about forgetting my driver's license, as soon as they turned their backs to look up my info in their computer, I gunned the engine and sped away.

The next few minutes were like a car chase out of a movie: slamming the accelerator, pounding the horn, weaving in and out of traffic—before finally crashing into the side of a house.

That's when I reached for the gun.

But it got stuck as I tried to remove it—jammed somehow. I yanked and yanked, but it wouldn't budge. Then the cops yanked *me* into their cruiser.

Fast-forward to a six-month sentence in an adult jail because of the severity of my crimes. I tried to keep to myself and stay out of trouble, but old habits die hard, and eventually I ended up getting into a fight that landed me in solitary confinement. Finally, after spending almost seventy-two hours alone in my underwear, Brian, a guard, entered my cell.

"Come on," he said. He led me to a side room, ushered me inside, then locked the door. I looked around at the room, realizing that this was one of the few areas without cameras.

My heart was in my throat. Brian stared at me, and after a long pause, he asked a simple but profound question:

"Dan, why are you here?"

"Well I got in a fight with Kirk at breakfast—"

He cut me off. "No, I mean, why are you in jail?"

I stammered, offering a few feeble answers: "I stole a car. I ran from the cops—"

Brian interrupted me. "No, Dan. I've been here for almost ten years, and I've met a lot of kids. *A lot.* But I see you trying to do your homework and stay out of trouble. You're different. It doesn't make sense to me. *You* don't belong here."

Hot tears came pouring down my face as Brian explained that he thought I was "meant for something else." Until that day, I'd only ever heard what a troublemaker I was. But somehow Brian saw potential in me. And his words gave me hope for a better life.

Looking back now, I can see that throughout my troubled childhood, I had *always* shown potential: I was creative, I was willing to take risks, I was good at talking to people, and I could deal with the chaos around me without losing my cool. In essence, I had shown the necessary skills to be an entrepreneur—but my skill set just hadn't been pointed in the right direction.

My next stop proved to be pivotal. Not long after my conversation with Brian, I was sent to Portage, a therapeutic facility for teens. There, my transformation continued. I studied and worked hard at the tasks I was given. Along the way, I befriended a maintenance guy, Rick, who became like a big brother to me. One day, I was helping Rick clean out one of the abandoned cabins when I found a book on Java programming sitting next to an old computer. I opened it up and what I saw shocked me. I had always thought computer programming would look like hieroglyphics, incomprehensible lines of complex math equations. But this . . . *this* read like plain English. And it spoke to me.

So I powered up the computer and typed in commands, following the simple list of instructions from the first chapter of the manual. Minutes later, the program ran and these words appeared:

"Hello World!"

That was it. Something just clicked for me. Here was a way to create a set of instructions that allowed me to get the same reliable and predictable results. Every. Single. Time.

The predictability of software counteracted the unpredictable chaos I had been living with my whole childhood. From that day forward, writing code became my new addiction.

I soon found myself obsessed with designing software and systems. Even today, when I teach clients to create systems for their companies, it's a huge thrill to help people turn chaos into predictability.

At the time, I was naively proud of myself—I didn't realize that "Hello World!" is the first lesson in every beginner's programming book. With unfounded confidence, I dove headfirst into this new advent, "the Internet." I took the same skills that had gotten me into trouble my entire childhood and pointed them full force toward entrepreneurship.

In fact, my chaotic childhood proved perfect for the world of self-employment—the unknown just didn't scare me. I opened my first legitimate business, a vacation rental site called MaritimeVacation, in 1998, when I was just eighteen. At twenty-one, I started my second business, NB Host, a hosting company for Web applications.

Entrepreneurship had redeemed my life and given me direction. But there was one problem. I knew only one thing: GSD—Get. Shit. Done. Work hard, make money, stay out of trouble. Day after day. Until my first two companies failed, miserably. I hadn't learned how to work well with other people or value my time. But starting businesses was in my blood, and I knew it. So I powered on, starting my third company, a software firm called Spheric Technologies, in 2004. There, my hard work began to pay some dividends—at least professionally. I was working fifteen-to-eighteen-hour days, which produced 150 percent of year-over-year growth—while simultaneously tanking my personal life.

Four months shy of my wedding day, on a seemingly normal day when I'd been working since the crack of dawn, I came home late in the evening to find a very upset fiancée.

"I can't do this anymore," she said, dropping her engagement ring on the counter.

Apparently, my once future wife thought that if I wanted to spend my life with her, I had to actually spend *time* with her.

Although I didn't realize it at first, my two failed businesses and my failed relationship all had one thing in common—*me*. And at the heart of my problem was my GSD mentality, which blinded me to everything else. I knew I needed to find a better way to run my businesses and my life.

Little did I know, the seed to my solution had already been planted.

A few years before my fiancée had left, I'd already started reading more business books. I'd picked up the audiobook version of *Love Is the*

Killer App by Tim Sanders. After reading—or rather, listening to—the whole book, I thought, *Wow. I just downloaded twenty years of life experience for $20 and a few hours of my time. How many more of these books can I get my hands on?*

After that, I started devouring the classics, such as *How to Win Friends and Influence People* by Dale Carnegie, *Think and Grow Rich* by Napoleon Hill, and *The 7 Habits of Highly Effective People* by Stephen Covey. These books had helped my business run more smoothly, but it wasn't enough. I needed to run my *life* differently. I needed systems that would supercharge who I am—an entrepreneur—while also helping me be a good person. Losing my fiancée was the wake-up call I needed to get serious about finding a true, holistic life solution. I kept reading, searching, and experimenting. I found secrets here and there about how to reclaim my life, live my passion, and own a business that didn't own me. I began to apply principles, tactics, tools, and systems from books, mentors, programs—any source I could find. And I started seeing results:

I began learning how to *do* what I love (lead businesses) and *be* who I want to be (a friend, father, and husband). I learned that I can't possibly separate entrepreneurship from myself because I *am* an entrepreneur. I sold Spheric in 2008 and made my first million, which completely changed my belief in what's possible. Then, I moved to San Francisco in 2009 to start my next venture, Flowtown. I kept building teams and infrastructure that freed up my time and energy so I could reinvest them. Oddly, this time, the more my company grew, the *more* time I had. I'd found a way to grow my company and my time simultaneously. And then I discovered something even more profound.

What brings me real joy is seeing other entrepreneurs find those same truths.

A core principle of mine is: learn, do, teach. You don't learn without doing, and once you've really learned something valuable, you should pass it on. Today, I know from personal experience, amazing mentors, and coaches who've helped me that the *only* way to grow your business past a certain point is to buy back your time and redeposit it where it matters most.

In 2006, I started a blog to share some of the growth tactics I'd learned. I wasn't an expert on buying back my time, but still, I just wanted to pay it forward with the little that I had learned about growing companies. People started commenting on my posts. Then, in 2008, I started giving speeches at conferences. These were mostly directed at fellow software companies. In the beginning, I usually discussed business tactics—like growth marketing strategies I had learned in the heart of Silicon Valley—but I was always more interested in helping the entrepreneurs and founders *live*. From all my blogs and conferences, I learned that I was not the only entrepreneur struggling with the GSD mentality, and it only strengthened my commitment to service.

In 2012, Flowtown was acquired, and I immediately started Clarity, a marketplace where we connected startup founders with the answers they needed for their new businesses, from startup advice to legal questions to marketing strategies. Again, I knew from experience that I owed all my success to the books I'd read and the advice I'd received. Clarity seemed like the perfect way to bring founders and their quest for answers together: at Clarity, leaders pay a fee to hear advice from experienced entrepreneurs. I knew that there were some real, deep questions that founders had, and when they got the answers they needed, they could unlock magic throughout their organizations. When Clarity was acquired in 2014, I went looking for my next challenge.

By 2015, I'd started SaaS* Academy, a YouTube channel for software company founders where I began freely sharing not only business tactics, but more intimate strategies—like valuing energy management over time management, the importance of company playbooks (standardized operating procedures), and, ultimately, how to buy back your time. I was amazed at the feedback—"Felt like succinct therapy," and

---

* SaaS is an industry acronym for "software as a service."

"This is the best breakthrough video I've ever personally watched." Apparently, I had stumbled on a near-universal truth: we all struggle with finding ways to juggle our time and our business.

Born entrepreneurs have to find a way to live fully, in their business and in life.

If you've been eating the GSD fruit for some time now, you've probably found some success. Hard work, even at the expense of your relationships, will pay off, to a degree.

But at some point, success will stall. You're one person, with a finite amount of time. You have a company, family, and friends, who are all demanding it.

If you find yourself dreading work—because you know you have a stack of emails to respond to, new fires to put out, and a dozen clients, customers, and employees waiting to dump work on your lap—and then dreading coming home—because you're exhausted, stressed, and still thinking about all that's left at work—then this book is for you. This book is for anyone who wants to buy back their time to do more of what they love while they grow their company. You won't be fully alive without being an entrepreneur, because it's in your DNA. But if your company's killing you, your family, or your relationships, with tasks that are eating all your time and energy, you can't go on like this. So don't. I'll help you find a better way.

This is the story of how I changed my approach—and how you can do the same.

How to Build a Business You Don't Grow to Hate

Stephen Covey once said, "The key is in not spending time, but in investing it."[1] Inside this book, you'll find *exactly* how to do that. You'll find a systematic approach, with tactics and strategies synthesized from two failed companies, a lost fiancée, reading over 1,200 business and self-help books, running the largest SaaS training and mentoring group in the world, and giving numerous talks on buying back your time.

Not only do I personally use everything taught here, but so have thousands of other founders and entrepreneurs who've learned how to buy back their time and energy and redeploy them correctly. As a result, they have more energy, feel excited about the future, and they love their businesses again. At work, their employees are happier. At home, they're better friends, parents, and spouses. Oh, and their companies have grown exponentially.

Most entrepreneurs think that a profitable business sprouts from hard work. That may be true, but a thriving *empire* only comes when the leader—you—learns how to buy back their time. Take back the reins of your life, enjoy your work again, and reclaim the freedom your business can provide you.

Trust me—I now know not only is it possible to have free time, live as an entrepreneur, and pour energy into your relationships, but that these are all intertwined—a happier Dan is a better entrepreneur, and a better entrepreneur is a better father and a more loving husband.

I've helped hundreds of other founders learn how to redeploy their time: to buy it back and deposit it where it matters most. They've learned that the more time they spend on what they're best at in their company, the more energy they have and the more money they make, allowing them to buy back *even more* time. It's the exact *opposite* approach I had in my first few companies, where the more my businesses grew, the more I suffered, only to eventually lose my company and my relationships.

I found the solution I was looking for, and I want to teach it to you.

Here's a brief snapshot of how this book is laid out:

First, I'll teach you the Buyback Principle, the Buyback Loop, and the DRIP Matrix. These mental shifts will allow you to rethink how you're spending time in your company. You'll learn how to quickly identify what's zapping your time, and why. Just by giving yourself a mirror, you'll see the insanity of how most entrepreneurs—maybe even you—are running their companies. You'll uncover the psychological limitations to your success, starting with your own Time Assassins.

Using the Replacement Ladder (chapter 5), you'll learn how to infinitely scale up your tasks and time with the next most valuable tasks. In chapter 7, we'll talk about creating replicable playbooks to pass on to your employees so that you maintain total control over your business without having to ever touch most of it.

Throughout the book, we'll explore how you can learn to play your own infinite game. We'll dive into the only three time trades that you can make.

There will be some quick tips and hacks along the way. For instance, you'll quickly learn that *every* entrepreneur can afford to start off-loading some tasks immediately (using their Buyback Rate; chapter 1). I'll also teach you how to design your own personalized Perfect Week (chapter 8) around *your* energy. We'll dive into easy tricks, such as the Definition of Done and the 1:3:1 Rule (both in chapter 9), that will help you overcome bottlenecks in your organization that are stalling your productivity. (Oh, and probably my favorite tip is the Camcorder Method, in chapter 7. This will help you train others without spending additional time. Check it out now if you want a sneak peek.)

By the end, I'll have you dreaming again (using a process called the 10X Vision map, chapter 13). Plus, I'll show you how to create the Preloaded Year (chapter 14) so that you can execute on that big dream. There will be homework you can do along the way, and I've collected all the material for you in one convenient place at BuyBackYourTime .com/Resources.

*

LEARNING HOW TO buy back my own time has created an incredible life. This week I'll spend six hours growing my eight-figure business.

I'll train for an Ironman. I'll volunteer with inner-city youth. I'll write my next book. I'll look for my next investment. I'll give my attention and resources to the at-risk entrepreneurs who give me so much energy and joy. Best of all, I'll spend time with my kids, eat lunch with my wife, and the four of us will enjoy dinner together . . . every night.

None of that has come because I simply grinded harder. All of it has come because I learned to think and act differently inside my company, so that every moment invested *in* it has allowed me to withdraw more energy *from* it.

And none of it came on my own—others guided me, authored books, hosted conferences, hopped on calls. I learned from them, and now I want to share all that information with you, in fourteen chapters.

In the end, this isn't just about you. This is about the future of your business, your employees, and your community. If you burn out, you'll burn down their lives as well.

Let's build a business you don't grow to hate.

CHAPTER 1

How I Buy Back My Life

Goals are about the results you want to achieve.
Systems are about the processes that lead to those results.

—JAMES CLEAR[1]

BY THE TIME STUART FOUND ME, he was in the fight of his life.

"I can barely leave the house, I can't take a full breath, and I'm having panic attacks regularly. I'm living a nightmare," he told me.

A few months before, Stuart had led a major re-architecture of the backend code that powered his company's apps. He worked fourteen-hour days, seven days a week, to see the project through. They finished by Christmas, so Stuart took a few days off to bring his wife and her sister to Disneyland. After ten minutes of walking through the park, he felt dizzy, his chest was tight, and he couldn't breathe. He found a bench to rest and assured his family, "I'm fine. Go on. I'll catch up."

Stuart wasn't fine. His heart and mind were racing. *Am I having a heart attack at the happiest place on Earth?* he asked himself. Eventually, Stuart got off his bench and rejoined his family.

But when he returned home, reality came knocking, and his symptoms returned. Medical tests revealed his heart was fine. The real problem? *Anxiety.* This puzzled Stuart because he'd never once had a panic attack, until now.

Soon he was having them twice a week. By March 2020—three short months after his nightmare at Disneyland—Stuart was in bed most days, paralyzed by his body's fight-or-flight response. His physical state was so low, even joining video calls (which COVID-19 had made standard by then) was impossible. Stuart did everything he could. He studied self-help books, tried meditation, and even forced himself to exercise, which was exhausting in his condition. Nothing worked.

Before Disneyland, Stuart was a young and enthusiastic entrepreneur: a thirty-four-year-old, well-educated, hardworking businessman. He studied finance in college, worked on Wall Street, and started his second company (which developed a suite of applications that helps small businesses increase online sales) in 2015. Within four years, he had ten employees, a dozen apps, and more than 640,000 active daily users. By most accounts, he was successful.

Like many good entrepreneurs, Stuart was immersed in the details of his company. He tackled most tasks himself because "that's how you get things done right." Plus, he had the expertise to back it up. In college, he'd taken accounting, so he knew how to keep the company's books. He also knew how to code, so he touched every piece of his software developers' work. He even booked his own travel plans and scheduled his own meetings.

Stuart had built a successful company, piece by piece. Using his intellect and prior experiences, he'd laid the foundation for an enterprise that provided for his family, employed others, and created value in the marketplace. While there were long days and sacrifices, it had all seemed worth it. Until now.

At thirty-four, everything came to a grinding halt. His body had said "Enough is enough." Now his company's growth seemed in jeopardy, and everything he'd worked hard to achieve seemed as if it were resting on a crumbling founder who could barely get out of bed.

I've been able to work with hundreds of interesting people, mostly entrepreneurs who are passionate about their companies. Sometimes, I'm helping them scale their sales teams, or coaching them on finding top talent or where to spend their marketing dollars. More often—and this is what I really love—I'm helping entrepreneurs find what's eating up all their time and energy. Once we unlock that together, I can help them get back to what's lighting them up and bringing them money.

But when Stuart, the founder of multiple software companies, came to me in 2020, he wasn't just looking for a growth strategy, a marketing plan, or even a way to save time, money, and energy.

He was looking for a way to save his life.

Breaking the Toxic "Get Sh*t Done" Mentality

A UC Berkeley study showed that entrepreneurs are significantly more likely to report a lifetime history of depression, ADHD, substance abuse, and bipolar disorder.[2] Most of us founders start our companies with good intentions—to provide solutions, to disrupt the market, or to spend more time with family and friends. With all these plans for a better future, why are *we* struggling with a litany of physical and mental health issues?

The answer?

We've subconsciously slipped into a pit of deception: *The more I work, the more productive my business will be.* On the surface, this makes sense. Work hard, stay ahead. That's the enticing part—the reason we get tricked. But over time, a hard-work ethic can lead entrepreneurs to believe one thing: more input, more output.

Simple busyness can't be the secret ingredient to business success. A hamster on a wheel is awfully busy. So is a dog digging a hole. I can think of more than one entrepreneur who spends hours a day running errands, being interrupted by team members, processing emails—they're certainly *busy* all day, but there's not a lot getting done.

Even *efficiently* staying busy isn't the answer. Most entrepreneurs are extremely efficient. They can eliminate task after task faster than anyone else. They can make the calls, send the emails, seal the deals—overall, they can *make it happen*. But efficient busyness on the wrong tasks simply creates a faster streamline to Stuart's situation.

When I met him, Stuart had convinced himself that hiring and training others required too much time, energy, and money. Tackling most tasks himself was easier and, to him, the most efficient way of ensuring things were done right. So he did everything. Why not?

Stuart wasn't just the bookkeeper and accountant; he was also the chief engineer, the lead project manager, the head of fulfillment, the head of customer support, and his own personal assistant.

His high standards and insane work ethic were undeniable, even admirable. But he was working seventy-hour weeks during an average month and hundred-hour weeks when duty called. Which is why he had an anxiety attack half a block from Sleeping Beauty's castle.

He didn't know how to reclaim his time and deposit it where it matters most.

The little-known secret to reaching the next stage of your business is spending your time on only the tasks that: (a) you excel at, (b) you truly enjoy, and (c) add the highest value (usually in the form of revenue) to your business. Likely, two to three tasks fit that description. Every other task you're handling is slowing your growth and sucking the life from you, and you should clear it from your calendar.

Yes, someone else should be handling about 95 percent of your current work so you can get back to what matters.

Allan Dib, author of *The 1-Page Marketing Plan*, said it like this:

> *You can always get more money, but you can never get more time. So you need to ensure the stuff you spend your time on makes the biggest impact.*[3]

If you're stuck in the grinding force of emails, phone calls, and putting out small fires, this probably sounds ridiculous. But stay with me.[3] For just a minute, forget whether or not what I'm saying is *possible*, and instead just consider how you'd *feel* if you were only executing what you're better at than everyone else, what you truly love, and what adds a crazy amount of value to your business.

Chances are, you'd breathe a huge sigh of relief. Your mind would probably clear. You'd probably be a better spouse, a better parent, and a better friend. Your employees would be happier because you'd come into work refreshed, steering the company toward bigger, better, and more inspirational goals, allowing each of them to flex their own professional muscles. Take my real estate friend Keith.

Keith was successful in his real estate company—no one in his area was as good at buying and selling homes as him. The problem? He was spending around twenty hours a week on calls, even at home. Finally, he solved the problem by hiring a salesperson on a commission-only basis (common for this situation) to field these calls. Keith's business grew, his wife was happier, and someone else made a commission. Now, Keith handles just 10 to 15 percent of the most important calls. And all that extra time? It goes to more valuable parts of his business and to his family.

Then there's my friend Martin—a fantastic business consultant who hired himself out to other businesses, helping them optimize their overall sales process and marketing strategies, among other items. His issue was that every week he had to do ten live calls, one in the morning, one in the afternoon, to help clients fix and improve their Facebook ads that were underperforming. After a while, he hated it. "I'm answering the same questions over and over and over again, on every call." It was draining him, and, worst of all, it was distracting him from the other areas of his business. But Martin's a creative genius—finally, he partnered with someone who fielded those calls *for free* because they offered a complimentary service, and they were delighted to hop on calls with prospective clients. Martin has freed up several hours a week that he can now redeploy back into the most important parts of his company.

Where can Keith and Martin spend their additional time? On what matters *most*—in their company, and in their lives. By transferring draining tasks, they free up the one asset that's invaluable: time. That time should only be spent on the most important tasks. The truth is, Keith, Martin, and Stuart have all realized that they're only really truly great at a few key aspects in their company. Time spent elsewhere is draining (and ultimately costly). What they must do is use their money to buy back more time. That's what the Buyback Principle is all about:

1. How to <u>spend</u> the most finite asset your business possesses: *the founder's time*
2. How to <u>invest</u> that time into what will bring the founder *more energy* and *more money*

The Buyback Principle means you should continually use every resource you can to buy back your time. Then, fill that extra time with activities that light you up with energy and make you more money. Notice the emphasis isn't simply on "hiring," but on hiring with a purpose: reinvestment. Stuart had employees already, and he was so stressed he felt like he was dying. The problem was that Stuart hadn't hired specifically to buy back *his* time.

With that in mind, here's how I formally define this whole concept:

> **The Buyback Principle: Don't hire to grow your business. Hire to buy back your time.**

This concept will not only grant you more financial success than you thought possible, but with it, you'll also be able to craft the life you originally envisioned when you became an entrepreneur.

You'll learn how to use this principle to buy back additional time in your calendar to focus on what makes you money and lights you up. And then a wonderful cycle begins: as your company makes more money, you buy back even more time. The result: you'll be happier, and you can continually upgrade your time and buy back your freedom.

As people pay you to do what you love, your energy goes up and you make more money, redepositing it back into what you're excellent at. Your business grows. As you'll find out in the book, you can keep hiring out those additional pieces that are must-dos, but not for *you* to do—administrative work, customer delivery, follow-up, even sales. As more work comes in, and you stay focused on what you enjoy, your business will pull in more revenue.

> The Buyback Principle means that entrepreneurs shouldn't be checking email unless they want to.

> The Buyback Principle means you excel at a few tasks, and you're mediocre at best at the others.

> The Buyback Principle means that when you're choosing what to do today, you should be selecting the highest-value tasks.

If you don't believe me, I get it. Most entrepreneurs don't. Stuart didn't either. Until he tried it.

The Rest of Stuart's Story

When Stuart finally got ahold of this Buyback Principle and started focusing on those areas that were most important, everything changed.

While he was largely bedridden and struggling to take a deep breath on a daily basis, this hardworking, problem-solving founder found my material and devoured everything I taught, over a two-week, video-watching binge.* For the first time, Stuart saw the lunacy of how he was running the company. More importantly, he saw a better way forward.

---

* On my YouTube channel, SaaS Academy.

He immediately began auditing his time, and what he found was remarkable. Stuart shared with me, "I've always been mindful of my time. But when I wrote it down, I realized, *Oh! I shouldn't be doing this.*"

Besides the shocking number of low-value tasks that were eating away his days, he was spending a ton of time scoping, managing, and completing engineering tasks. When he tallied his Buyback Rate (something I'll teach in the next chapter), he was shocked: there was a huge gap between the hourly value of his time ($100) and the hourly value of the tasks he was spending his time on ($10). Essentially, he was *costing* his company $90 an hour most of his workday.

And he was killing himself in the process.

Stuart prioritized what tasks to off-load next (I'll show you how to do this using the Replacement Ladder in chapter 5). Then he spent the next month filming himself with a video camera, recording himself conducting every task that he wanted to transfer to his two new hires (a trick we'll discuss in chapter 7, called the Camcorder Method).

Stuart learned what to off-load, what to keep, who to give it to, and how to manage everything. He learned that his entire goal wasn't to manage *productivity*, but to manage his own energy and emotions, maximizing his Production Quadrant (chapter 2) so he could bring huge results to his organization, all while getting truly excited about his work.

Within two months, Stuart freed up more than thirty hours a week, going from working eleven hours a day to working six, making him a more engaged father and a more supportive husband. He even found time to return to his former hobbies, such as earning his blue belt in jujitsu.

In the end, his company's revenue tripled, his income doubled, and his panic attacks disappeared, all in less than a year.

"My only regret," Stuart told me, "is that I didn't find you sooner."

Stuart's life perfectly illustrates how to buy back your time in a nutshell: entrepreneurs should use their resources to purchase more time. *All* this extra time should go toward those tasks they excel at, they enjoy, and that add high value to their business. Today, when Stuart thinks about hiring a new employee, he follows the Buyback Principle: *Don't hire to grow your business. Hire to buy back your time.*

Hitting the Pain Line

Stuart's story is a bit extreme. However, the path that led him there is one most entrepreneurs tread far too often.

Entrepreneurs who continue believing that everything rests on their shoulders—especially the low-value tasks they hate performing—will eventually hit the same point Stuart did. Something breaks. It could be their health, their morals, their family, or simply their daily habits. As I was writing this book, *three* of my new coaching clients came to me with stress-induced shingles or adrenal fatigue.

Some founders stuck in this grind self-medicate the daily stress with a variety of vices, ranging from the seemingly harmless to the clearly addictive. If you're an entrepreneur, you know what I'm talking about—maybe you overeat, game into the early morning, or veg in front of the television. If you've been in this longer and dealt with the stress for decades, you may have turned to much more harmful activities to get your head "clear" from the daily tasks that are haunting you.*

Entrepreneurs who don't learn to take back their week and refocus their energy will feel less and less free as their business grows because they come up against what I call the Pain Line.

The Pain Line is the point at which growth becomes impossible. For Stuart, that happened at Disneyland on vacation. Before vacation, he was a fast-paced diligent entrepreneur. After vacation, his body quit on him.

His Pain Line crept up on him physically.

If you're like most entrepreneurs, the Pain Line occurs right at about twelve direct reports and just over $1 million in revenue. At

---

* Yes, some turn to overeating, alcohol, and even white powder.

that point, you've built a business on your hard work ethic. Even if you have employees, all the stress is still on you. "The buck stops with me" is your mentality.

This work-hard, "no one can do it like me" mentality works. Until it doesn't. You can sustain growth up to a point. But then the emails, the to-dos, the low-value tasks you hate doing continue sucking your energy—it all creates a wall of pain. You realize that the more you grow, the more pain you'll experience. Your calendar will explode, and the weight of your responsibilities will increase. You think about work constantly, and you dread going in.

After coaching and leading thousands of entrepreneurs across various organizations (and experiencing the Pain Line myself), I can tell you this: no entrepreneur will grow into pain.

An entrepreneur will *ruin* their business before letting it grow into something more painful. They may do it subconsciously, and they may do it slowly—just enough—to bring the pain of their growing company back to a manageable amount of difficulty.

When you hit your own Pain Line—where the daily pain of working on tasks and projects you hate is too great—you either change (by embracing new beliefs, systems, and tactics) or you stop growing. Your growth halts because of an emergency (as it did with Stuart), or, more likely, you subconsciously stop your own growth by doing one of three things:

1 | SELL

When an entrepreneur is experiencing so much pain in their business they just want out at all costs, they'll often decide to sell.

For example, in 2020, a couple called me. They'd grown their business to $6 million in revenue per year. It was very profitable, but they hadn't learned to apply the Buyback Principle. After ten years, their health had degraded, their friendships were in shambles, and their marriage had turned into a roommate relationship.

They were done, and they asked for my help to sell. I explained how they could begin buying back their time to get their life back. But I was too late—they'd lost their passion for their company and their marriage.

Entrepreneurs can grind so hard that their drive and passion for their businesses diminishes to extinction. If you truly want to sell, sell, but on *your* terms. Don't just sell because you feel desperate to get out of a bad situation.

2 | SABOTAGE

Any of this sound familiar?

- You suddenly decide to launch a new product or line of business.
- You urgently feel the need to overhaul your website.
- You keep replacing key team players for small mistakes.
- You drag your feet on business decisions until the opportunity slides by.

If any of that sounds like you, you may be hitting your Pain Line.

Under pain, many entrepreneurs will make a subconscious decision to sabotage their own company because growing means more pain. It's a tricky one to see at first. On one hand, they desire to grow their business, and they're actively trying to, but every time they hit the Pain Line, they make a bad decision that knocks their business back into a manageable state, using that decision as the excuse. They don't realize that they're causing themselves to stop growing. Determined, they get back up, but the next time they hit the Pain Line, they make another bad decision, repeating the cycle.

Entrepreneurs don't usually recognize when they're self-sabotaging. Every time they reach their Pain Line, they sabotage their company's growth until it gets back to a level they can safely oversee. They make sudden decisions: "We need a new website." "Let's try changing markets." "You aren't doing this right!" They may justify these actions, but they're really just overreacting to internal emotions. While no one wakes up and says, "I'm going to ruin my business today," they *subconsciously* ruin their business by rationalizing unnecessarily dramatic decisions.

3 | STALL

Stalling is what happens when you confess, *I'd rather have a smaller company.* It's making a *conscious* decision not to grow. When you're so overwhelmed managing your current company's size, growth can feel downright exhausting.

Here's the dirty secret about stalling: a decision to not grow is a decision to slowly die.

Marketplaces evolve because human nature forces them to. Susan will always want a faster bicycle. Kevin will always want a better iPhone. Larry will always want a bigger TV. That growth-bent DNA expresses itself throughout every human decision. Even if you're a small business in a local market, if you don't evolve, your customers will leave for a better option.

Growth isn't just necessary for expansion. Growth is necessary for survival.

Perhaps the worst possible outcome of stalling isn't just your *customers* leaving you, but your *employees* leaving you. When you decide to stall growth, you start a countdown timer on how much longer your star players will hang around. The same nature that drives little Susan to want a faster bicycle is the same nature driving adult Susan to want a promotion, more money, and greater responsibilities in her career. If she recognizes there's no opportunity for her to grow at your company, she'll eventually walk away.

When you stall, even though you may not realize it, you're agreeing to shrink.

*

IF YOU CONSIDER TOMORROW – and you feel the dreaded weight of emails, administrative tasks, people management, and a list of activities you hate doing—you're facing pain. But here's the hope:

The Pain Line is your opportunity to change your perspective from thinking that *more business growth = more pain* to knowing that *more business growth = more freedom.*

Don't believe me. Believe Stuart.

By applying the Buyback Principle and redeploying his time, he now has more energy, and his company makes more money. He has more time with his family, and he employs more people.

He looked at his time and saw that how he was using it was a bit . . . crazy. He was stressing himself and hurting his relationships. Ironically, while he probably *thought* he was helping his company, he was hurting it. For one, he was not spending his valuable time on what would bring his company the most money. Second, by doing too many tasks himself, he was keeping others (like the head of engineering he ultimately hired) from getting paid to do work they're world-class at performing.

Stuart became the hero of his own story—he transferred tasks to people who were better equipped to handle them; then he started working on what he loved: building his company. And his business exploded.

Systems > Goals

I'm going to guess you probably already know that if you had dozens of extra hours in a week to focus on what you *really* wanted to focus on in your company, it would explode. You're smart, you have plenty of ideas on how you can arrange your company, increase sales, and up your marketing game. You've got dozens of ideas on how things could run smoother. But the problem is, you think:

I don't have the time.

I can't afford the help.

No one's as good at the work as I am.

No one wants to do the work.

I can't find good people to hire.

Basically, you know that with more time, you could create a better company. But these obstacles and others are standing in your way. What you need is a system. Trust me—I had guidance getting to the point where I am today, leading and investing in dozens of companies while *loving life* and spending time with my family. I want to give you that same guidance.

In *Atomic Habits*, author James Clear talks about the importance of systems versus goals. "Winners and losers have the same goals," he writes. "You do not rise to the level of your goals. You fall to the level of your systems." In this book, I'm offering systems to help you climb out of the first part of Stuart's story and land in the second part.

No one sets out to become an overstressed workaholic with declining health and relationships. Entrepreneurs end up there because they lack tested systems that deal with the unique challenges founders face.

In the chapters that follow, I'll lay out exactly how to climb into the best part of Stuart's story. The first thing you need is to understand how the Buyback Loop works.

The Buyback Loop: Audit-Transfer-Fill

When you use the Buyback Principle to repurchase your time, and then focus that free time on what lights you up and makes you more money, you create what I call a Buyback Loop.

> A Buyback Loop occurs as you continually
> <u>audit</u> your time to determine the low-value
> tasks that are sucking your energy. Then you
> <u>transfer</u> those tasks, optimally, to someone
> who's better at them and enjoys them. Lastly,
> you <u>fill</u> your time with higher-value tasks that
> light you up and make you more money. Then
> you start the process over again.

Did you catch it? Audit, transfer, fill. Using this approach, you can continually upgrade your time throughout your entrepreneurial journey, again and again. Today, the low-value tasks that are sucking your energy might be invoicing or emails. Once you've off-loaded those and upgraded your time and energy, you may start working on new marketing projects to get more customers or have the time to get on sales calls that you enjoy. Eventually, you'll likely need to move from there to working on your leadership or your company's strategy. Even from there, you can continue to spiral *upward* to build a business that feels effortless. Moments of pain are often the perfect opportunities to upgrade our thinking and begin a Buyback Loop that changes our life.

If you look around, you can see examples of the Buyback Loop in the lives of many of your entrepreneurial and artistic heroes:

Tom Clancy, one of the bestselling novelists of all time, employed writers to produce dozens of books under his name over the last two decades of his career. Meanwhile, Clancy served loosely as a front-end guide to conceptualize the stories and spent more time exploring exhilarating and lucrative new opportunities as a film producer and creative consultant. See the trend? Clancy started out as an author, then as his company grew, he transferred some of the work to others and kept growing and exploring in his own life. Clancy created a Buyback Loop (audit-transfer-fill, audit-transfer-fill) to go from writer to storyteller to film producer.

The Buyback Loop

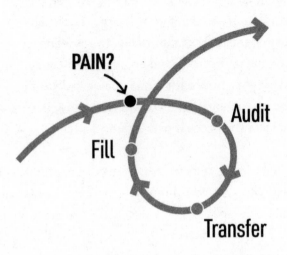

Pain often provides a choice—here, you can either continue on as usual or use audit-transfer-fill to upgrade your thinking and your life.

Or look at Warren Buffett. He spends his time on two primary tasks: reading books and searching for the next investment opportunity. His Berkshire Hathaway empire is approaching $1 trillion in value and employs nearly four hundred thousand people around the world. Of course, he didn't *start* there. He worked his way up in the financial world, starting early on as a salesman. Along the way, he was transferring tasks to others, upgrading his time, and moving upward.

Andy Warhol employed an eccentric group of ambitious artists and muses who helped him conceptualize and create his world-famous art. Over time, he began off-loading much of the lower-value portions of his artistic endeavors to other artists inside his studio, the Factory. He came up with ideas, then off-loaded much of the middle portion of the work to other artists. Then he came in at the end to sprinkle on his magic. Over time, he created thousands of pieces of art. Whether he called it that or not, Andy Warhol used the Buyback Principle to become an iconic artist whose legacy continues to this day. (We'll talk more about Warhol and the Factory in chapter 5.)

The simple audit-transfer-fill methodology creates an infinite cycle, so you can continually upgrade your time throughout your entrepreneurial journey.

I'll never disparage hard work or tell any entrepreneur that work ethic isn't a key component of success. You'd laugh at me. But I will say that you've got to couple a great work ethic with buying back your time.

Here's how to start thinking *audit-transfer-fill* in your day-to-day, beginning right now.

> **Audit:** *What tasks do I hate doing that are easy and inexpensive to offer someone else?*
>
> **Transfer:** *Who do I have on my team—or who can I hire, even part-time—to take these over?*
>
> **Fill:** *What tasks should I focus on that I love doing that can immediately bring more money to my company?*

Audit-transfer-fill is a simple expression of the Buyback Principle, but it offers a quick insight into what may be driving you crazy today.

As we continue our journey, I'll offer more specific systems on how to buy back your time. But for now, just remember these three key words: *audit, transfer, fill.*

*

STUART WASN'T A bad business owner. He was doing well, and he was highly competent in accounting, coding, and sales. Wearing all these hats may be inevitable at an early stage of your company. You can ride out the early days of a startup with all those hats on. But sooner or later, you'll reach a point of growth where you hit a wall and your individual efforts will no longer create the growth your business needs, and you'll either stop the growth by selling, sabotaging, or stalling, *or* you'll learn to overcome that pain by shifting your strategy. I suggest the Buyback Principle.

The Buyback Principle is what has allowed Stuart, Keith, Warren Buffett, and dozens of others that we'll learn about take hold of their life and build a business that the more they grow, the more freedom and income it generates.

That's what's in your future, beginning now. Just look around and audit how you're spending your time. Likely you'll find dozens of tasks someone else could do. Transfer those tasks to them. Then fill your time with something that gives you energy and makes you more money, beginning an infinite loop *upward* where the more money you make, the more you can buy back your time.

Rethink how you see your business. Time is the currency, the vehicle allowing you to purchase what you love or what you hate. If you purchase more work that you can't stand, well, you'll build a business of pain. If instead you constantly think of trading additional money to buy back your time, you'll grow a company that you'll love, not one that you'll want to escape from.

*

AT THE END *of each chapter, we'll end with the five hottest takeaways, followed by an application section called "Step into the Arena," which will give you a jump start on applying the ideas discussed in the chapter.*

5 Buyback Rules

1. The Buyback Principle: Don't hire to grow your business. Hire to buy back your time.
2. *You can't personally outwork yourself to a better business.* The problem is you only have twenty-four hours a day. Eventually, if you're

doing everything, you (or one of your relationships) will break down.

3. If you keep grinding, you'll eventually hit the Pain Line, where you're experiencing so much pain when you try to grow that you'll do one of three things: stall it, sabotage it, or sell it.

4. When you hit the Pain Line, it should act as a feedback loop—this is your opportunity to embrace a new mindset or to continue on in the status quo, waiting for something to snap.

5. A Buyback Loop occurs as you continually <u>audit</u> your time to determine the low-value tasks that are sucking your energy. Then you <u>transfer</u> those tasks, optimally, to someone who's better at them and enjoys them. Lastly, you <u>fill</u> your time with higher-value tasks that light you up and make you more money. Then start the process over again.

The Buyback Loop

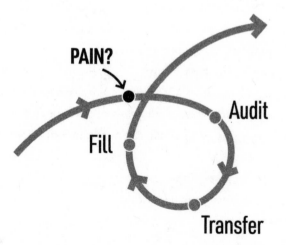

Pain often provides a choice—here, you can either continue on as usual, or use audit-transfer-fill to upgrade your thinking and your life.

Step into the Arena

Every time I share my screen in a Zoom conference call, someone points out the picture of the ripped guy on my desktop background. Sure, it gets some laughs in meetings when people see it, but it also motivates me to continue to work out every day. Because I see it so frequently—about a hundred times per day—I'm constantly visualizing what I'm after, and that future vision motivates my present.

For this chapter, I want you to envision your life without the barrage of to-dos and all the menial parts of your business you hate doing. I want you to know what you would do if you could buy back all that time. Ask yourself one question:

What would I fill my time with if I wasn't spending all of it at work?

I get it—right now, that may not seem possible. Forget whether or not it's possible, and just consider what you would fill your time with. Write it down. "If I had ten extra hours in a week, I'd spend it with my kids." "If I had an extra day in my week, I'd join a yoga class."

Do it, right now. Get a pen, and write it down.

If you want to get really fancy, you can take this up a notch by getting a "vision board" of what your life might look like with that extra time. To make a vision board, get a bunch of images together—a picture of you and your kids playing baseball together, a photo of someone in a yoga class, a drawing of you jet skiing across the water, et cetera—and put it all together. If you want to get an idea how others have done this, you can go to BuyBackYourTime.com/Resources to see some examples.

Whatever you do, just get the picture in your head, with words or a tangible image of what your life *will* look like once you've bought back your time.

CHAPTER 2

The DRIP Matrix

OPRAH WINFREY HAD A ROUGH childhood. She bounced between her grandmother, her mother, and the man she calls her father, Vernon. As a young girl, she was abused. As a teenager, she had an unplanned pregnancy. Those were just a couple of the many troubles she faced as a young black girl and teenager in the 1960s.

In her twenties, she landed a job as a news anchor in 1977. But the next year, she was demoted. Apparently, she was the wrong color.[1, 2] The network had hired her, then kind of fired her, then "didn't know what else to do with her," so they put her on a not-so-well-rated talk show.[3] Her demotion proved to be exactly what she needed.

Her first interview wasn't exactly the caliber of *Larry King Live*. No presidents, kings, or other heads of state. Instead, she interviewed Tom Carvel, the "Ice Cream King," and an actor from a soap opera. This type of interview wouldn't typically produce Earth-shattering revelations. But for Oprah, it was a turning point.

After her first show, Oprah knew: *"This is what I'm supposed to do."*[4] Before, when she was reporting news stories, she'd felt as if she were taking advantage of the people she interviewed by using their personal lives to sell news. But when she got real, into people's lives, she connected with her own calling. "The moment I did that talk show, I felt like I could be myself."[5]

From there, Oprah crushed it. You probably know pieces of the rest of her story. She eventually went on to found *The Oprah Winfrey Show*, won forty-seven Daytime Emmys,* was named "Queen of All Media," and became one of the first black billionaires on Earth.

It's hard not to like Oprah. She may be a celebrity now, but many people feel they know her. Because, after all, she just seems like a *real* person. She's had significant struggle. Even after she rose above her rough upbringing, she still faced adversity. But when she found the thing that gave her more energy than anything else, her life transformed, and her world ignited. She went from a news reporter to a world-renowned talk show host, who went on to become one of the richest self-made women in the world. She's inspired millions and built an empire, and she's loving every second of it.

Math Class or Art Class?

What Oprah found when she did her first talk show host interview is what author and psychologist Gay Hendricks calls "the genius zone." In his book *The Big Leap*, Hendricks divides up the tasks that workers perform during a day. He suggests that when entrepreneurs are executing tasks in their individual zones of genius, they're able to apply their unique, innate talents, and it's the "entry gate to the garden of miracles."[6]

Hendricks is speaking about those few activities that you know better than anyone else, give you immense energy, and the marketplace rewards you handsomely for. The more time invested there, the more money you'll make. But most entrepreneurs spend their time in the

---

*Likely, she would have won many more, but she stopped submitting her show for the award.

exact opposite way, on tasks that are sucking their time and energy and making less money.

When Miguel, a coaching client of mine and the entrepreneur of a real estate software company, used the audit-transfer-fill idea to plot his low-value tasks, he realized he was drowning in customer support tickets: "I'd been obsessed with getting back to people and solving their problems as quickly as possible."

Like most entrepreneurs, Miguel had built a business that was revolving solely around him and his expertise. Instead of staying focused on the area where he could drive the most value, he got caught up in low-value tasks that ate up his day. Luckily, he hired someone to lead his support team, "someone way more empathetic than me," who genuinely loved dealing with customers. Not only did their customer service ratings stay up, they went *through the roof.* Importantly, Miguel can now refocus his time and energy on what his customers need most and what makes more money.

"I'm actively working to identify areas where we can grow, because I want to operate at the ten-thousand-dollar-an-hour level, not the ten-dollar-an-hour level."

We all have our own areas that we not only excel in, but that we love and make us the most money. It doesn't make sense for a world-class wedding photographer to spend hours invoicing clients, or for a top-notch financial analyst to spend hours a week planning their own travel. Instead, these people would make more money (and be far happier) by finding someone else to do those tasks. The beauty is, genius zones change from person to person.

Remember that class you hated as a kid? For some, it was biology. For me, it was math. I hated math. Every second there sucked the life out of me.

On the other hand, we all had that one class that lit us up. In that class, time flew by. Mine was art class. Every moment spent at the drawing table boosted my motivation and energy to create. One minute, I was taking out my pencil, and the next, the bell was ringing, forcing me to stop. One could barely call it schoolwork for me. It was playtime.

Which class do you think I did better in, math or art?

Bingo.

Research backs this up. A study by Columbia and Harvard showed passion combined with perseverance predicts higher educational scores. Researchers studied thousands of GPAs, and what work students were most excited to perform. Their findings were simple: the more students enjoyed something, the better they performed. While perseverance was key in their findings, they noted that "perseverance without passion isn't grit, but merely a grind."[7]

When we apply this to entrepreneurship, we find an interesting correlation. It's obvious, but we too often forget it: our passion is where our marketplace value lies. The more we give ourselves permission to clear our calendar to invest in projects that light us up, the more our business will grow. We just need to learn how to get unstuck from the day-to-day work without having the wheels fly off.

Jack of One Trade

My brother Pierre started a home-building business in his twenties. He started out as a self-described "jack of all trades," applying for permits, paying bills, rolling out the tools at 7 a.m. for his carpenters, and rolling everything back up again at 5 p.m. I was an early investor. About six months into his new venture, Pierre called me and asked me to come over.

"Can you meet me at my house?"

"Sure. What's going on?" I asked.

"Well . . . it's better if we talk in person," he responded.

When I walked in the door, my mouth dropped. I hadn't seen Pierre in a while, and he'd lost about twenty pounds. When I looked around his home, *all* his furniture was missing. "Pierre! Did you get robbed?"

"No, no . . ." He started to stammer. "Look, I don't know what's wrong, but the homes aren't selling."

With two homes completed, a third being built, and no revenue rolling in, Pierre was in dire financial straits. He'd refinanced his own home, maxed out three personal credit cards, and moved all his furniture into a model home, hoping that staging it would help it sell. On the floor of his bedroom was a sleeping bag and a leaky air mattress that he shared with his dog. Each night, he pumped it up, and each morning they'd wake up on the hard floor again.

My brother is a brilliant salesman. When we were kids, our dad ran a popular fish-and-chips food truck in the summer months. Eight-year-old Pierre watched all those customers queue up in the sun and calculated that about half were only buying cold soda. He figured people who didn't want to wait were walking away, so he dragged a cooler next to Dad's truck and sold icy cans of pop, making up to $300 in a single day. At twelve, Pierre bought an old car, restored it, sold it, then used the money to do it again. By sixteen, he'd made enough money fixing and selling old cars to buy himself a new one—a shiny white Mustang GT. Like I said, a brilliant salesman.

At his house, I tried to offer Pierre some reassurance. "Pierre, don't worry. We're going to figure this out."

His main problem was his jack-of-all-trades mindset. He'd been so busy picking up hammers that he'd neglected his unique gift: sales.

After our meeting, Pierre spent time in the mindset of what he does best—sales—and that's when he finally understood his target customers. He quickly realized that despite the great build of his houses, they had no curb appeal, no landscaping, no finishing touches, no splash of color or warm lighting—all important factors to the key decision-makers in home purchases (usually women). He eventually hired an architect to redesign his homes with large windows, functional kitchens, and great bathrooms. As a result, he went from almost going bankrupt to selling sixteen houses in his second year. Over time, Pierre learned to delegate and specialize to the point where

Martell Custom Homes became the largest custom-home builder in all of Atlantic Canada.

It bears repeating: you have unique gifts that create real value. Clear out your calendar so you can practice those gifts.

How to Get Paid for Your Genius

The Pareto Effect suggests 80 percent of all results come from 20 percent of activity. The accepted 95:5 rule makes the numbers even more dramatic for entrepreneurs, suggesting that only *5 percent* of everything you're doing is driving *95 percent* of your company's returns.

That means if you spend ten hours at work today answering emails, making calls, talking to employees, going to meetings, developing content, only *thirty minutes* of what you're doing is driving tangible results in your business. What's worse (as the Columbia and Harvard study showed) is when you don't enjoy something, you're also not as good at it. In other words, while you think you're sacrificing for a worthy cause by working hard at things that challenge you, you're actually *costing* your company. It's a lose-lose move. I know, because I've been there (see Introduction!).

Think of every task as sitting on two continuums: one of energy, one of money. Each task is sucking some amount of energy from you on one end, or lighting you up with lots more energy on the other end. Meanwhile, that same task makes you somewhere between no money and lots of it.

When the overwhelming majority of your tasks are in the bottom left corner, making you little money and sucking lots of energy, then you're living a pretty chaotic lifestyle. Until Oprah discovered her biggest value to her audience—explaining human-interest stories—she spent her time in the news. There, she felt like she was exploiting her audience, not serving them. She made less money and simultaneously disliked her job. It wasn't until she realized her gift was shining a light on other people by interviewing them and sharing their genius with the world that her whole financial world exploded.

Until Pierre tapped into sales, he was in the wrong mode as well. He was busy with lots of activities, but none of them were making him money, and all of them were costing him energy. He kept working harder and harder, but he kept doing less and less of what he loved. Again, the result wasn't a huge payoff. Quite the opposite. By letting go of his passion for sales because of day-to-day work, he wound up in debt and almost went broke.

When you look at your own entrepreneurial journey, if most of your activity today is creating little value and also sucking the life out of you, then inwardly you probably feel chaotic and a bit in despair.

The Billionaire's Day

Oprah is now living what most people only dream of. In 2018, she did an interview with *Harper's Bazaar*. By then, she was one of the richest women in the world and seemed to be loving her life. She gave a detailed look at what an average day looks like for her[8]:

- **7:01 a.m.:** Wakes up surrounded by nature at her home in Montecito, California.
- **8:00 a.m.:** Brushes teeth and takes her five dogs outside. Makes her favorite espresso.
- **8:30 a.m.:** Enjoys a series of spiritual exercises like meditating, reading, and silence.
- **9:00 a.m.:** Works out for an hour.
- **10:30 a.m.:** Private shopping with Brunello Cucinelli in her living room.
- **12:30 p.m.:** Eats lunch and sips a glass of rosé in her garden with Stedman (her partner) or a friend.
- **1:30 p.m.:** Spends two hours on business matters, mainly approving

any expense over \$100,000 and checking in with Gayle King, *O* magazine editor-at-large, and Mindy Grossman, CEO of Weight Watchers.

- **3:30 p.m.:** Exercises again, then enjoys fresh tea and a good book.
- **6:00 p.m.:** Eats dinner and walks her dogs again. Occasionally, she enjoys a good movie.
- **9:30 p.m.:** Takes a luxurious bath, then goes to bed.

I hope you caught it: Oprah spends only *two hours a day* on traditional business matters. She spends the rest of her time on health, discovery, and personal growth. She knows that her highest value is remaining a compelling, insightful resource for her audience and remaining open-minded to discovery. (She also seems to be having a helluva lot of fun.) By focusing her time and energy on what makes her a valuable asset to her enterprise, she's built multiple media companies and has amassed a net worth of almost \$3 billion. She's making lots of money, and doing what lights her up.

You'll find the same is true in other highly successful people's lives, regardless of field or industry.

It's easy to think, *They're lucky*, or *They're privileged*. But the truth is, they built their lives following the Buyback Loop, investing time where it matters most, and reaping the rewards.

Tom Clancy, Warren Buffett, Oprah Winfrey, Andy Warhol, and entrepreneurs like Miguel, Stuart, and thousands of others have all learned how to effectively focus their time and energy where it counted the most. This unlocked immense value for themselves, freed up their time, and injected their lives with joy. As a result, they made more money, which allowed them to buy back more time. With that additional time, they made sure to deposit it in places that lit them up and made more money. To me:

Successful people aren't doing what they love because they're rich.

They're rich because they've learned to do what they love, and *only* what they love.

Too many entrepreneurs get this backward. They think that an enjoyable life is only for those who've earned their way there. So they grind, taking another bite out of the GSD mentality.* If that's you, you'll never get to Oprah's status until you bust that mindset.

You can only get to Oprah's level by starting to act like Oprah *today*. You may not have her money (yet), but you have some amount that you can spend to off-load the most time-sucking, energy-draining tasks. You start by changing your mindset and looking for ways to:

- Audit your time to find time- and energy-sucking tasks that others can do
- Reinvest that time in money-making initiatives and activities
- Set aside time to grow your business
- Invest only in tasks that make you the most money and light you up

The DRIP Matrix

Oprah was spending all her time on what lights her up and makes her money. If we borrow from that concept to create four quadrants, we get what I call the DRIP Matrix.

I use the DRIP Matrix to show people how they're spending their time. If you're spending all your time in the bottom left, the Delegation Quadrant, you're doing tasks that should be removed from your plate as soon as possible. Contrast that with the opposite corner, the Production Quadrant. Here, you're spending your time on what matters most, which is what brings you insane energy, lots of money, and drives your business forward.

Let's break each quadrant down.

---

* GSD = Get shit done.

The DRIP Matrix

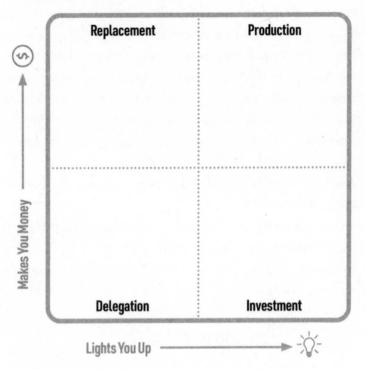

The DRIP Matrix allows you to see how valuable a task is, in terms of money and energy. The goal is to spend the majority of your time in the Production Quadrant, with some deposits into the Investment Quadrant. In general, you want to remove tasks in your Delegation Quadrant **as quickly as possible.** Removing tasks in the Replacement Quadrant takes more time. A system like the Replacement Ladder (chapter 5) can help ensure that you don't get stuck in this quadrant.

Delegation

MAKES YOU LITTLE MONEY, DRAINS YOUR ENERGY

Tasks in the Delegation Quadrant are menial tasks that are sucking your energy. Think about administrative work, billing, invoicing, setting up travel arrangements, responding to emails, et cetera. I know millionaires who are still performing many of these tasks because they just haven't figured out how to get rid of them. They have beliefs around them that keep them a prisoner of that work. What they don't realize is that they could be much more successful if they just audited their time, transferred those tasks, and filled their day with higher-value and rewarding work. Instead, they're bogged down by the weight of it all.

Tasks in the Delegation Quadrant should be found and quickly moved on to someone else when possible. Think about it this way: If you paid a marketer $100,000 a year, would you want them spending six hours a day cleaning the office windows?

If you're doing tasks that bring in very little money *and* they're draining you, you have one simple goal: transfer them as quickly as possible.

Once, my marketing team at SaaS Academy came to me with a problem. They needed to transfer a ton of data from one system to another, and it was going to take dozens of staff-hours. My team was really worked up about taking time away from other projects that could make us hundreds of thousands of dollars, for what was essentially data processing. I quickly looked online and found someone else who was an *expert* at this exact sort of data migration, who was happy to take the work for less than $1,000. Likely because they were an expert at it, it would probably take them half the time it was going to take anyone on my team, and they'd do it twice as thoroughly, as it's all they do day in and day out.

In chapter 4, we'll unpack how to do a Time and Energy Audit to find what's stealing your time. Then you'll know exactly what to get rid of, giving you some quick wins that will help you accelerate out of the Delegation Quadrant. By putting in a little strategic effort, you can start to feel more freedom in your life and less like your business day is a hurricane. (If you want to start eliminating these tasks now, look around and ask yourself, *How can I audit-transfer-fill?*)

Replacement

MAKES YOU MONEY, DRAINS YOUR ENERGY

Here, you'll find highly important tasks like onboarding, selling, marketing, and managing your team. These tasks are high value, but they may not light you up the way they once did, so it's less obvious what you do with these tasks.

In terms of priority, the Delegation Quadrant contains tasks that you need to get rid of ASAP. The Replacement Quadrant contains those tasks and areas of responsibility that may take a little more thought to outsource.

Typically, once you know what's in your Delegation Quadrant, you can transfer those tasks almost immediately for very little money. Think about administrative tasks, emailing, research, travel, et cetera. But tasks in the Replacement Quadrant will need more care (think sales or marketing) and typically cost more to get rid of.

Some entrepreneurs, once they've eliminated the lowest-value tasks, still end up never reaching their fullest potential in the Production Quadrant. They end up stuck in Replacement because they have a mound of tasks that cost substantial money to outsource, and they aren't sure where to start.

That's why, sometimes, I call this the pitfall quadrant—you can get stuck in here, working on sales or marketing or delivery or managing big teams, because these tasks *do* make you money, but they *don't* light you up. These tasks are better to do than working on low-value tasks that neither make you money nor light you up, but I want you to shoot for something higher, something better. I want you to shoot for Oprah or Buffett.

Founders often think that they must do everything—it's the "right way" to run a business. That's what my colleague Larry thought.

Larry owned a healthy grocery store—you know, like Sprouts or Whole Foods, just a little smaller. He was great at what he did, so his business grew. Eventually, he owned *two* stores. He was still rocking and rolling. Later, he expanded into his third location. It sounded like he was killing it, but that's actually when all his trouble started, and he started living out of the Delegation Quadrant. By the time I caught up with Larry, he was dreading his whole business.

"Dan, all I do is hire, fire, and order. I'm working like crazy, and it's miserable."

"Do you have an assistant, a store manager, or any sort of general 'number two' to help you out?" I asked.

"No. If I don't do it myself, it won't get done right."

I hear this sort of explanation all the time. I've been prone to thinking that myself. I asked Larry a simple question:

"Larry, name a brand in your industry you really respect."

He was pretty quick to respond with, "Whole Foods."

"Larry," I asked, "do you think the CEO had any help getting to their current size, or did they do everything themselves?"

Larry got where I was going. He was starting to see that things being done right is critical, yes. Those special little touches are often the secret sauce of your entire business, but they can be taught (I'll show you how, using the Camcorder Method in chapter 7), and *you* should not be doing all of them.*

Investment

MAKES YOU LITTLE MONEY, LIGHTS YOU UP

The Investment Quadrant (lower right) contains those tasks that light you up but don't make you much money, at least not today. Every task here is an investment—in yourself, in relationships, or in your business.

---

*We'll talk more about how to show others how to execute *exactly* as you want in chapter 7: "Building Playbooks."

For entrepreneurs, these activities are often highly collaborative and thought provoking—depending on your personality, this could include things like writing a book, speaking at conferences, being interviewed on a podcast, or going to lunch with peers in your industry. This quadrant also includes hobbies and health, such as wakeboarding, skiing, yoga, or playing chess. Any time you spend with your family, friends, or faith organization would also go into this quadrant.

Typically, tasks in the Investment Quadrant fall into these categories:

Physical activities: You can use hiking, snowboarding, and other workouts as incredible ways to connect with others, exercise for yourself, and have an opportunity to learn about your company, simultaneously.

Time with others: Any time you spend hanging out with friends, family, significant others, or in your community goes in this quadrant as well. There's no sense in getting through all of life and finding out one day that you missed the most important parts.

Hobbies: Think of biking, yoga, building model airplanes, painting, et cetera—all these endeavors belong in the Investment Quadrant. These are vital to keeping up your creative mindset. While no one may be paying you as you build a model airplane, you're exercising and building your creativity—a key ingredient in business. Think about how much happier you feel when you're pursuing your hobbies. Trust me—those around you can feel that. Hobbies are vital.

Industry collaborations: Here, I include things like podcast interviews, coauthoring a book, giving a TED Talk, et cetera. Unless you're being paid for the content creation itself, most of these activities don't make a lot of money *today*. However, most of them are investments in the future of your business. When you do a podcast interview, you're creating marketing material for your brand while also building potential client and partner relationships. When you coauthor a book, you're driving future clients to your company. Giving a TED Talk uplifts your entire brand.

Personal and professional development: You can add new skills by taking professional certification programs, studying, reading books, or going to school. You could also get a business mentor, attend a conference, or go to a personal development workshop. All of these are investments in yourself that will eventually pay dividends.

When coaching clients, potential partners, or even just friends who happen to be in town, one of my favorite things to do is invite them on hikes, a bike ride, out wake surfing, or for a run. This allows me to do a workout (investment in self), pour into other people's lives (investment in others), and oftentimes I'm spending time with potential coaching clients (investment in my business).

I also have a private Facebook group where a bunch of us challenge each other to commit to challenges like one hundred pushups in one hundred days or 75 Hard, an intense workout and personal development program. (When I was writing this, we had 230 people in our Facebook group!) I also have a snowboarding group, and I host entrepreneur dinners and lunches whenever I can.

Unlike in the despair or the Replacement Quadrants, the goal is to *always* have some activities in the Investment Quadrant that nourish your soul, your relationships, and flex your creativity. We aren't going to focus as much on the Investment Quadrant in the coming chapters, but I have a cheat sheet in the back of the book called "7 Pillars of Life" that you can use to score yourself.

Production

MAKES YOU LOTS OF MONEY, LIGHTS YOU UP

When most of your tasks are in the upper-right-hand corner, where you're making lots of money and your energy is flowing, you're living in true freedom. Here, you're highly energized, and the market responds by bringing you more money. As the market pays you and your company more, you have more money to buy back more of your time and energy, giving you more room to invest into what lights you up and makes you money, which makes you *more* money, creating the Buyback Loop we talked about in chapter 1.

This is where you want to spend as much time as possible—depositing time into the quadrant that only includes tasks that *both* light you up *and* make you insane money.

My buddy Chris is a fitness guru. He started out as a personal trainer working at a physical location. He used social media to gain more customers. Eventually, he was spending *two days a week* on social media, drumming up business, when what he wanted to do was help clients get healthy. So he had a choice to make: hire someone to help, or stall out. He hired someone, but—and here's the key—he hired someone *to handle the social media*. Why? Because that's what was sucking Chris's time.

Chris wisely wanted to deposit his time into the area that made him the most money and brought him the most energy, which for him was working with real people, helping them get fit and healthy. So he hired someone part-time to handle all the social media. Then Chris spent two more days with his customers. As a result of his social media efforts and his world-class training, word got out, and Chris's business grew. He tried to keep up with demand by raising his rates, but eventually it wasn't enough—his calendar was tapped out, and he'd raised in-person rates as high as he could.

That's when Chris went online with his training: he moved out of his physical location, and now he builds workout programs online, still working with customers on their fitness and health. In only five years, Chris went from having a few clients in the gym to making $1.5 million in annual revenue. He did it by continually redepositing his time into his Production Quadrant. As Covey says, "The main thing is to keep the main thing the main thing."[9]

The One Thing to Never Hire Away

All of this makes sense to most people—"Do what you're best at." So how do people end up spending all their time incorrectly?

Often, entrepreneurs accidentally paint themselves into a corner as their business expands. They start out doing what they love, and because they don't know *how* to hire correctly, they hire willy-nilly. "I need a videographer." "I need a marketing guru." "I need a podcast producer." And so on. What they often don't realize is that they're hiring out parts of their business that they do enjoy, and ultimately, they end up performing all the lowest-value work in the company, effectively becoming the company's administrator.

Of course you should hire help, but you should only hire help with the right mindset. Remember, the Buyback Principle tells you exactly *how* to hire:

Don't hire to grow your business. Hire to buy back your time.

Most entrepreneurs aren't thinking about *their time,* they're just thinking, *I need some help to get something done.* So you hire someone to help. The challenge is you now have another person to manage on top of all the work you were already doing. The way to grow is to START with your calendar (time).

Say you're a baker who loves making cookies. At first, it's a side hustle. But all your friends keep telling you that you should start baking for other people. So you do. You get some small clients around town, and as the business grows, you offer a couple college kids who love baking some part-time work. Every couple weeks, you tally up their hours and pay them. The business keeps growing. While they're baking, you're able to do the ordering, run to the store to pick up supplies, or throw up some pics on social media. Your business keeps growing. Eventually, you're not baking at all—you're doing payroll, ordering supplies, and managing clients.

When you think about going to work on Monday, you're already dreading it, because you're doing everything *except* what you love about your company—baking cookies.

That's what a ton of entrepreneurs do. Hiring is *absolutely* how you grow, but you must hire to *save your time*; otherwise, you're painting yourself *into* the Delegation Quadrant.

Remember, the goal is to stay focused on your Production Quadrant, constantly hiring to redeposit all your time there.

But before I talk about getting you some help with what's keeping you out of the Production Quadrant, let's tackle two objections I often hear:

"No one does it right."
"I can't afford it."

Let's break these limiting beliefs right now. We'll start with "No one does it right."

I get it—you think *you're* best at marketing, sales, coding, website design, ordering, hiring, firing, stocking the shelves, cleaning the floors, the administrative work . . . everything. *No one will do it quite right* is your mentality.

To be honest, likely no one *will* care as much as you do, because it's not their company, their money, or, really, *their* customers. Maybe no one ever will do it quite like you. So here's what you do. You don't aim for 100 percent perfection. Instead, shoot for 80 percent. *Yes, lower your expectations*, because here's the deal:

> **80% done by someone else is 100% freaking awesome.**

You not having to come in on the weekend to get caught up is 100% freaking awesome.

You not having to miss your kids' game or a friend's birthday party is 100% freaking awesome.

You not having to spend half your week doing something you hate for the hundredth time is 100% freaking awesome.

So that's why you need to set your bar at 80 percent done. If there's draining work on your to-do list, and someone else can get it done 80 percent of the way (and do it for the right price, which we will get into), then you should transfer that task.

That's how you'll get back to your Production Quadrant. As a bonus, when you really get the hang of hiring correctly, you'll be hiring people to take on tasks that live inside *their* Production Quadrants, meaning everyone is executing on tasks that they enjoy performing and make them money. (Sometimes you'll surprise yourself, and they'll not only be 80 percent as good as you are, they'll be even *better*.)

When you transfer what you dislike doing and take on more of what you enjoy that makes you more money, you immediately set yourself up to increase your revenue, allowing you to off-load even more of what you dislike. Over time, you continually push yourself up and to the right of the quadrant, in an infinite spiral upward. (Remember, the Buyback Loop.)

It's an eternal, never-ending game of business. You get to upgrade your time and hire someone else to take on tasks that you ultimately didn't enjoy. You take on more work that lights you up and pays you well. Then you make more money, moving you up again. Continue this loop and eventually you'll wake up, look around, and see that you've built the life, even the empire, you want.

In his smash hit *The Infinite Game*, Simon Sinek discusses the power of a never-ending approach to life and business: "Infinite games have no finish line, and the goal is to keep the game going as long as possible."[10]

> **While some entrepreneurs think, *One day,***
> ***I can stop this madness if I work hard enough,***
> **smart entrepreneurs think, *Today, I'll build a***
> ***game I want to play forever.***

I could have stopped working when I was twenty-eight, after I sold Spheric for millions, but I don't want to retire because I love what I'm doing. I love creating and building companies. I *want* to keep playing my infinite game. The more money I make, the more I can hire others to take on tasks that don't light me up anymore. The more I do that, the more money I make, and the better my life gets.

Okay, so that's objection one.

Now let's deal with objection two: "I can't afford it."

You Can Afford It

The first thing everyone does is say they *can't* afford anything. I disagree. Everyone can afford something.

Entrepreneurs can get fuzzy on how much their time's worth. Let me make it easy for you:

> **Your time is worth how much your business**
> **pays you divided by two thousand hours.**

As you probably know, two thousand hours is a normal work year. (Yes, I know you're probably grinding out more hours than that, but this is a rough estimate to help get you started.) When I say "pays" you, I mean all the profits from your current business—including your salary, discretionary expenses (wink wink), plus any other profits of the business after all expenses are paid.

If your company pays you $1,000,000 a year, then you make $500 per hour. If your company pays you $100,000 a year, you make $50

per hour. If you take in $24,000 a year, then you make $12 per hour.*
Until you learn to buy back your time from the low-value tasks and
start focusing on the high-value ones, you won't be able to build the
life you want. Learning how to make these trades is the game.

So that's how much your company is currently paying you. Now,
how much can you afford to pay someone else?

I'd like to introduce you to your Buyback Rate.

Buyback Rate Calculation

My rule of thumb is that no one—not a founder, not an administrative assistant, not a baseball player, not a barista—should be performing a work task that they could outsource for one-fourth (i.e., 25
percent) of their current effective hourly rate. So if your effective
hourly rate is $100 an hour, then your Buyback Rate is $25 an hour.
Why do I calculate your Buyback Rate as one-fourth of your hourly
rate? Because I want you to get four times your ROI when you're hiring someone using your Buyback Rate.

Let's take Tina, a small-business owner. Assume she makes $200,000
a year from her business. So her business is effectively paying her $100
per hour. One-fourth (or 25 percent) of that is $25 per hour, her Buy-
back Rate:

> What Tina's business pays her per year: $200,000
>
> Divided by 2,000 work hours per year: $100 per hour
>
> Divided by four, Tina's Buyback Rate: $25 per hour

To all my math nerds: You probably noticed that you don't really need
to determine your effective hourly rate to find your Buyback Rate. All

---

* $2,000 a month × twelve months in a year = $24,000 a year, divided by 2,000 hours =
$12 per hour.

you need to do is divide how much your company pays you by eight thousand—that gives you your Buyback Rate and skips knowing your effective hourly rate. So the simplest form of this equation is **what your company pays / eight thousand = Buyback Rate.** I'll break out the effective hourly rate to keep it less confusing for the rest of us ☺.

Every time Tina's doing something (like paying invoices or editing video) that she could have paid someone else $25 an hour to do, she's taking from her own company.

Some of you may be running into the issue that you already spend all the money you pay yourself, so you don't have anything left over. Well, that's the issue. Instead of leasing that new premium car, why not buy used and invest in a great executive assistant and work to trade that free time into the ability to get that brand-new car from the increase in profits?

Buyback Rate Formula

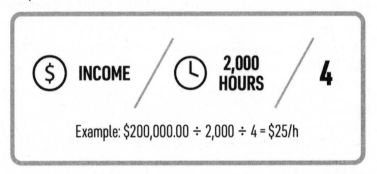

$ INCOME / 🕐 2,000 HOURS / 4

Example: $200,000.00 ÷ 2,000 ÷ 4 = $25/h

Everyone has a Buyback Rate. Even if you currently take in only $50,000 a year from your company, your Buyback Rate is approximately $6.25 per hour. Even if that's all you can afford right now, you still may be able to provide a useful job for someone. Other times, there are ways to get things done for free—remember Keith and Martin from chapter 1? They transferred sales calls to others without having to spend a dime because they were paid solely on commission.

Interns are a great source of talent that comes with low cost. In the early days of building my company, I would use students from the local college. It helped them gain experience, and it helped me buy back my time.

Did you know you can hire Web developers, administrative assistants, and social media experts in other parts of the world for less than $6 an hour? Search online, and you'll find many sites like UpWork that help you review, vet, and hire top-rated talent at affordable rates.

Throughout this book, I'm going to show you how to constantly increase your Buyback Rate, so you can buy back more and more time. When you have more money, you buy back more time, and deposit all that extra time into your Production Quadrant, where people pay you insane money. So the more money you make, the higher your Buyback Rate. Keep working to increase it. Turn it into a game.

No Time to Grind

When you find those few tasks that light you up, that make you money, why not put *all* your time there?

1. You'll get paid more.
2. You'll enjoy your work more.
3. You'll be giving someone else a job.

But far too many entrepreneurs spend their time grinding because they erroneously believe that they're the only person for the job, they can't afford any help, or they feel guilty not doing certain work. They may hire as they grow, but they aren't hiring to buy back their time. Over time, their day looks like a full list of to-dos that they never signed up for, and that also don't pay well. That's living in the Delegation Quadrant.

To get out of Delegation and into Production, start using your Buyback Rate today to transfer tasks.

Now, even with the right mental models, there are a few Time Assassins sabotaging your success that you must keep at bay. We'll tackle those in the next chapter.

5 Buyback Rules

1. Science shows that people perform better working on tasks they enjoy. Higher performance leads to higher pay.

The DRIP Matrix

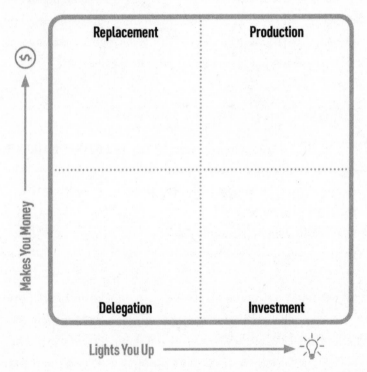

The DRIP Matrix allows you to see how valuable a task is, in terms of money and energy. The goal is to spend the majority of your time in the Production Quadrant, with some deposits into Investment. Generally, you want to remove tasks in your Delegation Quadrant *as quickly as possible.* Removing tasks in Replacement takes more time. A system (such as the Replacement Ladder; see chapter 5) can help ensure that you don't get stuck in this quadrant.

2. Every task you perform sits on two axes: one of money, one of energy. Each task brings you from little money to lots of money, and either drains you or brings you more energy.

3. Many entrepreneurs hire away the parts of their business they love the most. This typically happens accidentally—as they grow, they don't hire to buy back their time, they hire for a position or role, mistakenly making themselves the administrator of their own company.

4. 80% done by someone else is 100% freaking awesome.

5. The DRIP Matrix: Delegation (less money, drains energy). Replacement (more money, drains energy). Investment (less money, gives energy). Production (more money, gives energy).

Step into the Arena

This chapter's homework is simple:

Calculate your Buyback Rate.

To calculate your Buyback Rate, you first determine how much your company pays you. To do that, you add up *everything* that your company pays you—from profits, to salary, to vehicles, to fun trips—and then divide that number by two thousand. That's how much you make from your company per hour. Now, divide that number by four.

The result is your Buyback Rate. So, if you make $400,000 per year, then you divide that by two thousand hours a year, then divide by four, your Buyback Rate would be $50 per hour. That's the amount you can afford to pay someone else to do a task. From now on, there's no task you should be performing (that you don't enjoy) whose cost is less than your Buyback Rate.

CHAPTER 3

The 5 Time Assassins

HAVE YOU EVER HAD ONE of those perfect opportunities that just suddenly dropped into your lap, and no matter what your plans were, you couldn't say no? On a random Thursday morning in 2014, my friend Daniel Gruneberg sent me this email, and all my plans suddenly changed:

> "I wanted to take a moment and invite you on a ski trip to Verbier, Switzerland, with Richard Branson and some other entrepreneurs."

I'd just been invited to go skiing with my hero. Founder of Virgin Records, Virgin Atlantic, and 398 other companies, Branson has long been one of my entrepreneurial idols. We'd both been told we'd never amount to anything and gone on to found multiple companies. I'd poured hours into reading every book he'd ever written, watching every interview, and shadowing every business move. Now I would get to meet him in person.

The trip was only three weeks out. Normally, I'd *never* be able to get away last-minute like that. But in this case, I made it happen. After all, this was my hero, and you only live once.

As I packed my bags for Switzerland, I had a flashback from another trip with an entrepreneur friend, Lionel. At the time, he owned a forestry company with $2 million in revenue and sixteen employees. At that stage, you'd think he would've had his company running like a well-oiled machine. But the company was running him.

On my trip with Lionel, he'd spent our entire drive on his phone, barking orders and putting out fires. While the chairlift was pulling his body up, his mind was checked out, ticking off imaginary checklists. He couldn't even pretend to have fun. His company, with a handful of employees and $2 million in revenue, was sucking him dry.

If company size, revenues, and employees correlated to stress, Branson should have been about ten to a hundred times *more* stressed than Lionel.[1]

But from the moment I arrived at Branson's Swiss chalet, nothing could have been further from the truth. Every morning, Branson hit the slopes with us, laughed on the chairlifts, and cracked jokes throughout the day. He was relaxed, excited, and fully present. Frankly, he carried less stress than many of the other entrepreneurs visiting him. Other than Branson's one employee who joined us—his administrative assistant—nothing from work followed him into the powder.

> Lionel, with one company, $2 million in revenue, and sixteen employees: stressed as hell.
>
> Branson, with four hundred companies, seventy thousand employees, and billions in revenue: loving life.
>
> My question is: The next time you go on a ski trip, do you want to be Lionel or Branson?

The Chaos Junkie

About nine out of ten of the entrepreneurs I meet tell me they had a chaotic upbringing. Formal research seems to back this up. In a study, researchers at the University of Queensland in Australia found that children with challenging childhoods are more passionate about starting a business.[2, 3] Steve Blank—a Silicon Valley entrepreneur and Stanford professor—has a theory he calls "dysfunctional family theory."[4] He says that good entrepreneurs "have similar personality traits, including passion, tenacity, and a remarkable comfort operating in chaos."[5]

At SaaS Academy, I have all my employees take various personality profile tests to help determine what to look for in a future candidate—if all my top staff have a particular attribute, I know to look for that attribute in the marketplace when I hire. I take the test, too. Do you know what's right at the top of mine? "Ability to handle stress." That superhuman ability is what allows me to juggle all the aspects of the founder's life—a client doesn't pay an invoice, a huge deal falls through, COVID-19 messes up our current business model, we need to go into a new line of business, we must redesign the website, et cetera.

I'm sure you've seen this in your own life. When a key employee randomly takes personal leave, or when an internal mistake costs you thousands, your unique ability to handle stress and chaos allows you to thrive where others would struggle.

Likely, you can function extremely well even without a solid game plan—something that others struggle with. As an entrepreneur, you can probably show up to the office, and when a sudden change in regulations, staff, or clients means you have to move forward in the dark, you don't shrink back. In fact, you likely excel. Why? Because it's in your bones. If you had a chaotic upbringing, you were trained for this.

For many entrepreneurs, a chaotic childhood also meant that they've had practice MacGyver-ing their way out of situations others never experienced. If your guardians didn't pick you up from school on time, didn't get you to baseball practice with the right glove, or forgot to make you lunch, you solved getting home, finding a glove, and eating lunch all on your own.

If you grew up on the rough side of the tracks, from an early age you were probably learning street smarts and negotiating skills necessary to handle tough situations. These lessons, fair or unfair, gave you the problem-solving and navigational skills necessary for entrepreneurship: when others see an impossible situation, you can draw on years of your can-do spirit to come up with a solution from the fringes.

Steve Blank compared working in a startup to marines fighting in a war. He put it bluntly:

> *Startups are inherently chaos. As a founder, you need to prepare yourself to think creatively and independently, because more often than not, conditions on the ground will change so rapidly that the original well-thought-out business plan becomes irrelevant.*
>
> *If you can't manage chaos and uncertainty . . . and if you wait around for someone else to tell you what to do, then . . . you will run out of money and your company will die.*[6]*

If startups are "inherently chaos," then it makes sense why early childhood adversity can help build the muscles necessary to handle that chaos.[7] So that early childhood adversity you experienced? Probably a good thing.

I made a list of a few of the possible positive outcomes from early childhood adversity:

Chaotic childhood	Entrepreneurial enablement
Came home to a frequently untidy house.	You can function relatively well in a disorganized environment.
Forced to solve atypical problems, such as providing emotional comfort for younger siblings.	You have an ever-present, problem-solving mindset.
Weren't sure where your next meal was coming from.	You deal with the unknown with calmness.

---

* Steve Blank wrote this, but he was paraphrasing and adapting a military speech given by infantry officer Donovan Campbell in Campbell's book *Joker One*, his memoir of his time as a marine during the Iraq War.

Chaotic childhood	Entrepreneurial enablement
Couldn't depend on adults for basic needs (like a ride to soccer practice).	You can manage excess responsibility.
Dealt with abnormal childhood stress.	You can deal with high-dollar, complex problems.

Here's the bad news:

Entrepreneurs can also become so accustomed to stressful and unknown environments that they become downright addicted to chaos.

Chaos can feel so normal that calm can actually feel strange. Entrepreneurs have been so trained in dealing with stress, like making difficult decisions based on incomplete information and last-minute changes, that they're always looking for the next problem, even if it doesn't exist. Without a fire to put out, they can grow inwardly anxious.

I have a friend who sabotaged a multimillion-dollar business deal just because it was going so well, and he started freaking out. So he kept finding reasons to stall the deal, or make it not work. He wasn't even aware he was doing it.

Once you're so addicted to chaos that it feels normal, you can accidentally look for it everywhere. When you look for the problem, you often create it, which weirdly reinforces your belief. It's like the person who thinks everyone's staring at them, so they act fidgety and nervous, and voilà, everyone *is* staring at them.

Once, I was working on a deal with my business partner, Matt. I was getting frustrated because the team in charge of handling the deal's logistics was moving slow, at least to me. I told Matt I was ready to step in and handle it myself.

"Matt, I think I'm going to step in, take things over, and push this deal through."

"Hang on, Dan—do you think everyone on this team is horrible at their jobs?"

"No, of course not."

"Then you need to stay out of their way and let them do their work."

I was about to step in and push our team out of the way, a team that Matt and I had put our trust in. If I had stepped in, then I would have reinforced to myself that this was a fire that needed a hero, and that I was that hero, and no one else could ever handle the job as well as I could.

That's classic chaos addiction.

The underlying problem was *not* our team. It was *my* impatience and tendency to live in chaos. If this was allowed to manifest itself, I might have saved the day, but I would have robbed our team from learning how to handle the problem for the next time. And over time, I might have created a solid belief that no one could handle these tough situations but me. (Thank goodness for Matt.)

I try to be "Matt" for my clients.

So I force all new coaching clients to contact me before making any large-scale changes. Because I've seen clients cause problems when they weren't there, just because they felt an internal stirring to create a disaster. They randomly suggest overhauling their entire website. Or they suddenly fire a key employee. Perhaps just as their company starts to make solid margins on a product, they change directions. I call these hand grenades. And before I let a client toss one, I tell them to text me.

While I was writing this book, Taylor texted me. Following the Buyback Principle, he'd reorganized his time and his team. His company was running smoothly. So far, so good. Then he suddenly decided to go on a six-week unplanned vacation. Thankfully, he knew he had to text me first. I replied with two words and a question mark.

Instead of enjoying the peace (and the profits) of a well-*planned* vacation, Taylor just wanted to take off without warning. He couldn't let go of chaos. Once he left town, something would inevitably go wrong, requiring him to return and putting him once again in the role of firefighter, and, perhaps to him, all would be right with the world.

In this chapter, I'm going to try to help you see what I help all my clients see: *why* you may be acting a certain way. Many people in my life have held up a mirror to my actions, and now, because I know what to look for, I can spot my own chaos addiction when it starts to flare up.

We're going to dive into the five most common areas where a founder's chaos addiction presents itself. By the end, you'll be able to see yourself in one, or maybe several, of these Time Assassins.

The 5 Assassins That Kill Your Success

Overall, the subconscious need for uncertainty and chaos comes out in one of five ways, which I call the 5 Time Assassins to entrepreneurial success:

1. **The Staller:** You sabotage your own success by hesitating on big decisions.
2. **The Speed Demon:** You make rapid decisions, such as hiring the quickest/easiest/cheapest option. Then you find yourself in the same position again.
3. **The Supervisor:** You fail to properly train, micromanaging others, failing to empower them to grow and learn.
4. **The Saver:** You have money in your bank account but don't understand the value in spending it on growth opportunities. You let it grow like a nest egg instead of investing it in your business.
5. **The Self-Medicator:** You turn to food, alcohol, or other vices to reward yourself when you have success. Then you rush to the same destructive activities to escape failure or pain.

Let's break these down:

1 | THE STALLER

The Staller drags his feet when opportunities come knocking:

- "Want to host a webinar in front of an audience full of your target customers?"
- "I'm a distributor who can get you in front of ten thousand people. Want to connect?"
- "Would you like to speak at our next TEDx event?"

Think of all the scenarios that could help your business grow, like through an introduction, a new referral, a bigger audience. When these opportunities pop up for the Staller, they never take them, and they also never say no. They subconsciously outsource the decision-making to someone else, just like my coaching client Saheed did.

My team was researching potential partners in the marketplace who had a customer email list of at least fifteen thousand people in my target market. Saheed popped up, and my team gave me his name. I thought, *Oh! I know this guy.* Saheed was already a coaching client of mine.

I could get Saheed in front of my entire audience (and me in front of his), effectively tripling his reach with a simple introduction. This should have been a cinch—an easy win-win partnership.

"Should" is the operative word.

I fired off a quick email to Saheed on September 1:

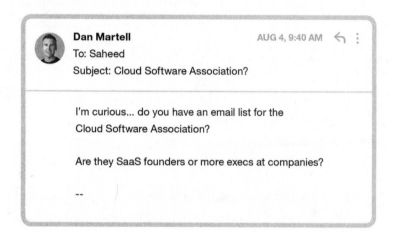

Two weeks later, that email sat in Saheed's inbox. I followed up. Still nothing. Oddly enough, Saheed hopped on a coaching call with me and other leaders, but he never bothered responding to this email. Finally, on September 21, Saheed replied. At this point, I couldn't partner with him, as that would mean recommending him to my trusting audience—and I couldn't in good conscience refer someone who takes almost three weeks to reply to an email. Saheed's a great businessman, but he was haunted by the Staller.

Something inside was probably telling him he wasn't worthy, whispering doubt in his mental real estate:

You'll fail.

You'll let Dan down.

You're not worthy of this growth opportunity.

This will cause so much growth it will suck the life out of you.

2 | THE SPEED DEMON

The second assassin is the Speed Demon. The Speed Demon makes you believe you drive success by making decisions as quickly as possible. When you are falling prey to the Speed Demon:

- You haphazardly hire the first candidate you find (whether it's an aunt, a friend, or the mailman).
- You forcefully select the first technology platform you find (even if it doesn't fit your needs).
- You go with the first lender available (regardless of other, better options).

The Speed Demon laughs as you do all this and more with little consideration of additional options. Here's what happens next:

- The employee you hired quits, underperforms, or gets fired.
- The technology platform you selected doesn't work as anticipated.
- The lender you went with becomes a pain in the ass.

Charles is the head of one of the companies in my portfolio. His CMO happened to be his brother-in-law, and I'd noticed a few of his decisions that concerned me. I asked Charles about it: "Do you think your brother-in-law is a world-class marketer?"

Charles didn't even bother answering me. He just laughed. He admitted he'd been underperforming for a while, so he made the difficult choice of firing him and immediately replacing him with his buddy Darwin. No interviews, no shopping the market. "Darwin's the guy," he confidently told me. Two months later, Darwin quit out of nowhere.

I called Charles again and asked him about Darwin's sudden departure. It turns out, Charles and Darwin had been colleagues at a different company. There, Darwin had done *the exact same thing*—as soon as the job got tough, he left.

Charles had a classic case of Speed Demon-itis. He made a mistake, and then kept barreling forward without reflection, making the same mistake again. John Dewey once said, "We do not learn from experience. We learn from reflecting on experience."[8] Without stopping to consider *why* something happened, you're unlikely to fix the issue.

- If every employee you hire sucks, it may be your training.
- If every client has the same complaint, maybe there's a problem with your delivery.
- If you keep having the same business problems at the same intervals, it may be your strategy.

With an addiction to chaos, "every employee sucking" feels downright normal. You might complain about it, but deep down you feel like it's *normal* to have this issue. And if something's normal or expected, you won't reimagine the problem in such a way as to truly fix the underlying causes. You'll just keep on dealing with the symptoms. The problem is, if you lived in chaos when you were younger, you've built an expectation to live in chaos when you're older.

3 | THE SUPERVISOR

When you hire someone and then do their job for them, you're in danger of the Supervisor. The Supervisor is the opposite of the Speed Demon. Haunted by the Supervisor, you either micromanage others or just take over completely. I'm an avid mountain biker, and in my hometown, there's exactly one bike shop worth visiting—Daryl's. Every time I come in, Daryl jumps over his mechanics to greet me with a hearty, warm "Hey, Danny boy!"

He takes my bike, rushes off to the back, taps something, then . . . voilà! He hands my bike back to me.

His employees just stare. Without any explanation from their boss, they have no idea how he diagnosed the problem and fixed my bike. Every time they have an opportunity to learn something new, their boss inadvertently takes that opportunity away from them.

Daryl thinks he's being a team player, but the result is that he's robbing his employees from learning, and he's creating a never-ending dependency on Daryl. He isn't *training* for growth. He's *doing* for now. And because he's running his business that way, none of his employees understand what to do when he's not there—I've ordered several new bikes that never arrived, or arrived so late that I've had to go to a different bike shop. Overall, Daryl's too busy working *in* the business instead of working *on* it.

Here's the telltale sign that you're being haunted by the Supervisor demon: if you're thinking, *I'm the only one who can do it right*, maybe that's true. And that's a problem.

If you're lured by the Supervisor, you'll end up exactly where you are today—stressed and overworked. The path out is to recognize that you aren't the world's best at just about everything. You're only phenomenal at a handful of tasks. Everything else, you'll be surprised to find, someone else can learn and execute *at least* as well as you can.

4 | THE SAVER

The fourth assassin is the Saver. This one infiltrates the entrepreneur who's only saving money, not reinvesting it. Once the Saver gets ahold of you, you've created a false sense of success by hoarding a "nest egg."

In the summer of 2019, my buddy Kyle called me. He runs a multimillion-dollar mastermind for entrepreneurs, investors, and ideators. It costs over $40,000 a year just to join this monthly group, and he had almost fifty members when he called me, frustrated.

Every month he was re-creating a world-class event for his members, entirely from the ground up. The events were fantastic, but they required intense forethought and planning. Each one was themed around a current topic, and each month Kyle had to come up with that big idea. He wanted a sustainable way to execute events that didn't depend entirely on his monthly imagination. He was so worn-out, he was considering dropping the whole thing and closing up shop.

I asked him about his curriculum. He had *none*: no principles, no core concepts, nothing to work with. I suggested he talk to my friend Simon Bowen—a world-class ideator who helps leaders develop a curriculum around their expertise so they can systematically teach it to others. I offered to introduce them.

I told Kyle that he would probably charge less than $10,000 to help him put together a curriculum. But Kyle stopped me to ask, "Does he have a $20 book I can read instead?"

"No, he doesn't," I said.

"Hmm . . ."

Instead of spending $10,000, which was only one-fourth of one member's fee to join his mastermind, Kyle tensed up. He was willing to burn out and risk a growing, multimillion-dollar business to save a few bucks.

Kyle—likely addicted to chaos—was looking for a problem when it wasn't there. He was looking to "save," even though that wasn't necessary in this instance.

The problem with being excellent at fixing problems is that you'll want to fix them . . . even when they don't exist.

5 | THE SELF-MEDICATOR

In 2005, I *was* the Self-Medicator. By then, I was twenty-five and running my third business, Spheric, a technology company. Yale called. For me, this was ironic. I'd skipped college entirely, and I'd never dreamed of setting my foot inside such a prestigious institution. But now, Yale was asking *me* to set up their software programs.

I flew into New Haven, Connecticut, picked up my rental car, then called my dad to share my excitement.

After a day's work setting up their servers, I was ready to celebrate. I asked around about where I could grab some sushi (a rare commodity in my inland hometown of Moncton, New Brunswick). Everyone pointed me to the same place.

I ordered an abundance of sushi—and sake—to celebrate.

I celebrated for far too long.

When I woke up the next morning in my hotel room, I was still drunk. I called in sick. "Food poisoning" was all I could come up with.

In twenty-four hours, I went from hero to zero. That's what the Self-Medicator loads up on his victims, pushing people to self-sabotage to celebrate, and self-sabotage to escape. Whether you win or lose, the Self-Medicator wants to eat up your chances of success tomorrow. Land a huge contract? Drink. Lose a huge contract? Drink.

Whether you're overworked or bored, exhausted or exhilarated, escaping or celebrating, the Self-Medicator is happy to hand you a vice.

Give Life to Production

If you notice, each of the 5 Time Assassins is hurting your production in the long run for the sake of chaos, but in the immediate term they're zapping your time:

- The Staller won't let you move past big decisions.
- The Speed Demon ensures you keep making the same mistakes.
- The Supervisor ensures your time never upgrades, meaning you'll

spend more and more frustrating hours on tasks that you're only
mediocre at, at best.

- The Saver is tricky—he tells you to save your money, costing you
time. You agonize over a $100 purchase that could have saved you
ten hours.
- The Self-Medicator is perhaps the hardest to detect, as he often
sneaks up on you in the form of celebration. But a night of celebration can easily turn into sleeping in late, robbing you of precious hours of productivity.

Whether you're a billionaire, a millionaire, or a solopreneur who's just
starting out, you're prone to the 5 Time Assassins at any stage. Particularly as you find more and more production and have more and more
time available, the 5 Time Assassins, being the greedy little trolls that
they are, will try to zap any newfound time and energy.

Statistically entrepreneurs are more prone to having a chaos addiction. So as the 5 Time Assassins come for you, they'll disguise
themselves in justifications. You'll *think* you have reasons for acting
rashly. You'll feel the urge to fire an employee because "they deserved
it." You'll suddenly change your website because you want to "stay
fresh," or you'll overeat because "it was a long week."

Likely, it's just one of the 5 Time Assassins camouflaging themselves with faulty reasoning, enticing you because you feel the need to
jump into despair. I want you to recognize these moments for what
they are so the 5 Time Assassins don't steal away hard-earned time,
money, and energy.

The Alcoholic Millionaire

By the time I met Tom in 2018, he was running a moderately successful business.

He was making money, but he was also self-medicating (assassin
number five).

He was stuck in a binge cycle he'd picked up in his high school days. Beginning on Thursday or Friday, he'd start drinking until Sunday night, just in time so he could stagger into work on Monday still a bit drunk. He'd sober up for a few days, then start the cycle over again.

As you can imagine, his assassin was ruining his relationships. Once, he noticed his ten-year-old daughter chugging soda in the same manner he chugged alcohol. She mentioned how "fun" her dad was when he drank, and she wanted to be just like him. That stung.

A key turning point happened when Tom got real with himself. In one of our "Boardroom" meetings, which are my group sessions I host with my clients, Tom shared his struggle with alcohol. It turns out, Tom wasn't alone. "It was shocking," he told me later, "but I was no different than anyone else in the group. Everyone had issues they dealt with. Some with drinking, others with other issues."

After that vulnerable meeting, Tom started 75 Hard, an insanely difficult health and exercise program, something he'd tried before. But this time, Tom finished 75 Hard, and his life changed forever.

These days, Tom is one of the most disciplined people you can imagine: he wakes up at 5 a.m. every day and he's lost almost fifty pounds (down from a self-described "unhealthy 230"). Plus, he expects to have just shy of nine hundred employees in 2022, and his business is going to hit $15 million. But to Tom, perhaps the best accomplishment is that he can proudly and truthfully say this: "Now, I can go to a party, and I don't even think about a drink or wanting to drink. Feeling free is an understatement."

Were there ups and downs in Tom's journey? You betcha. But he's free today, all because he decided to face the mirror and get real with his pain.

Today, I want you to do the same. Get real with what's eating you. It may not be as big as Tom's demon, but my guess is there's something that's coming for you. Find it and get real.

Then nothing can hold you back. Your relationships, your health, and your business will all benefit from you dealing with your own chaos addiction.

In the rest of the book, we'll be buying back your time. But for now: Go get that assassin.

5 Buyback Rules

1. Research confirms what business coaches have observed for years: most entrepreneurs are addicted to chaos.
2. Your ability to deal with chaos gives you an entrepreneurial advantage, but can also make you subconsciously seek out chaos.
3. Your chaos addiction shows up as one of the 5 Time Assassins: the Staller, the Speed Demon, the Supervisor, the Saver, or the Self-Medicator.
4. Most people bounce from one assassin to the other without facing the root problem: addiction to chaos.
5. Becoming the person you want to be requires you to get real with any demons.

Step into the Arena

There's a popular Indian story about the mythical archer-warrior Arjuna. As legend has it, Arjuna was his teacher's favorite because of his outstanding ability with the bow.

One day, his teacher placed a small wooden bird in a tree, and then lined up his students. When he asked what they saw, each student mentioned various elements within the environment: the tree, the leaves, the teacher, the other students.

But Arjuna—who indeed shot the bird from the tree—only mentioned one thing: the bird. He saw right through the distracting issues.

I want you to have that same laser focus on the assassin you're currently facing. So:

1. Take out a sheet of paper and list your last ten major decisions, the ones that really shook things up.
2. Look at your list and ask yourself: *Were these all necessary, or were they hand grenades?*
3. Look for patterns in the decisions that weren't necessary. Were you rushing? Micromanaging? Penny-pinching?
4. Then, if you see a pattern emerge, write down your current assassin.
5. Bonus: If you really want to have fun with this, you could always print off a picture of a target and write in "The Supervisor" or "The Speed Demon" or whatever assassin you're currently facing. Then fold up that target and put it in your wallet or purse and carry it around with you.

Once you zero in on the assassin you're currently facing, you'll notice him the next time he tries to pop up in your psyche when you're about to make a decision. Like Arjuna, you won't be distracted—you'll know what you need to eliminate.

CHAPTER 4

The Only 3 Trades That Matter

WE TEND TO THINK OF people who end up like Richard Branson as "lucky," "wealthy," or "privileged." Any of these may be true, but in general, that doesn't take into account the capital-T Truth. Oprah achieved her monumental success not because she found luck, wealth, or privilege—she had next to none of those—but because she found *what lights her up*. Once she discovered the magic of talk shows, she dumped all her time and energy into that task. (I think we're all glad she did.)

Too often, entrepreneurs see the lifestyle that Branson and Oprah have, and they just keep grinding, thinking, *One day, I'll have that kind of freedom.* The truth is, as soon as you start depositing time into your Production Quadrant, you can begin reaping the rewards—you don't have to wait for "one day." Those rewards—more energy, more money—allow you to buy back more of your time, which can then be redeposited into the Production Quadrant again.

My friend Simon (mentioned in chapter 3) tells a version of the Buyback Principle with his own clients. One day, the owner of a manufacturing company, whom we'll call Andre, complained to Simon:

"I'm really sick of all the day-to-day stuff. I think I need to hire an operations manager."

"Okay, Andre," Simon said. "But before you do that, talk to me about your day. What's the biggest chunk of time you spend each week on something you hate doing, which just feels like work to you?"

It turned out Andre was spending 80 percent of his time on computer-aided drafting, or CAD, which is essentially drafting with a computer. Unless you *love* CAD—and some people really do—spending 80 percent of your time on computer-based drafting is a real drain. Talk about living in the Delegation Quadrant!

So Simon offered Andre a different solution:

"Andre, you *don't* need an operations manager. Instead, hire a *CAD designer.* Not only will that person be less expensive, but you'll get eighty percent of your time back."

Simon went on to mention that if Andre hired really well, the new hire would probably do a better job than Andre because CAD *is* something they enjoyed doing.

Simon was trying to get Andre to become a true entrepreneur. What Andre probably didn't realize is that he was still an employee—just an employee of his own company.

The Three Trade Levels

There are three trades available to everyone—you, me, Branson, and Andre alike—but most people never realize they're making them.

You can be a:

- Level 1 trader: employee
- Level 2 trader: entrepreneur
- Level 3 trader: empire-builder

Here's how they break down:

Level 1 Trader: Employee

AN EMPLOYEE TRADES THEIR TIME FOR MORE MONEY

Even if you own your own business, if you're trading your time for more money, you're an employee: you just happen to be an employee of your own company. You're using your time to purchase an income. Most entrepreneurs are firmly entrenched at this trade level. They're still living in the GSD mentality.

Everyone (unless you start out independently wealthy) begins their financial and business journey by trading their time for more money. They get a job, and someone pays them. When they own their own company, they typically start by selling their time as a software developer, a writer, or a window washer for a payday. Then they're still an employee, a Level 1 trader.

We've all been there, particularly in the startup days. But to grow so you don't hate your business, you can't keep trading your time for more money. There just isn't enough of it. We've got to take advice from Simon and start upgrading our trade level.

Level 2 Trader: Entrepreneur

AN ENTREPRENEUR TRADES THEIR MONEY FOR MORE TIME

Eventually, we must embrace trading our money for more time. When we do, we arrive in a new era of productivity, gaining leverage.

Here, you'll have shaken off the notion that more hours equals more money. You'll understand that your money can buy you more time to build the life you desire, the business you always wanted, and an empire few others can imagine.

As I've explained, this isn't as easy as just hiring more people. Done the wrong way, hiring more people will increase your workload. Rather, every time you make a hire, buy software, or complete a transaction, you should be asking yourself, *How do I buy back more time with this purchase?*

When you become a real entrepreneur (not just one in name), you've released the idea that more hours equal more money. Instead, you've embraced a better mindset: that, through delegation and replacement, money can buy you more time to spend on building the company and, ultimately, the life you desire. This is the essence of the Buyback Principle. Making it your MO begins with a critical acknowledgment that your time is either the engine or the anchor of your company. You must focus on only the most valuable tasks you enjoy. In other words, if your highest-value tasks are worth $500 an hour, you shouldn't be spending a single hour on a task that's worth $10 to your company.

We already talked about your Buyback Rate; now, I want to let you in on a little secret that I tell all my clients, something Simon was trying to get Andre to see as well:

> **$10 million companies were not built on $10 tasks.**

Level 3 Trader: Empire-Builder

AN EMPIRE-BUILDER TRADES THEIR MONEY FOR MORE MONEY

Players like Branson and Oprah have completely bought back their time. They're not just business owners. They're in another category altogether. They're building their own empires. They're the sole authors of their entrepreneurial journeys, and their time isn't even on the trading block anymore. They've found freedom.

Oprah works out more than she works. Buffett reads more books than financial statements. And both continue to make millions. Importantly, you never become a Level 3 trader without going through Levels 1 and 2 first.

Three Levels of Trade

At Level 3, your personal life gets *really* exciting: You have ample time for jujitsu or your kids' soccer games or walking your dogs or sipping espresso or eating lunch in your garden. At this level, other capable people run the day-to-day of your (probably multiple) businesses, and you have all the time you want to dream up new investments or opportunities. Your headspace is so clear and your energy is so high, you're thinking of how to turn good into great, some into more, and an investment into a bigger return.

The Quick Wins

Okay, so how do we get there?

Well, the first thing you can do is look for the quick wins, the items that are eating all the low-hanging fruit hanging out in your Delegation Quadrant. That's what Simon helped Andre do—Andre was spending all of his time on CAD. What are you spending all your time on that's likely in your Delegation Quadrant?

In the next couple chapters, I'm going to show you how to get rid of the tasks in this pesky quadrant and give you some quick wins so you can immediately buy back the lowest-value parts of your day. Importantly, you must know how much money you have to spend on buying back those items. That's why we calculated your Buyback Rate in chapter 2. Armed with that information, you can now begin to buy back time that's being spent in the bottom-left-hand corner.

Later, we'll talk about the more difficult tasks in the Replacement Quadrant. For now, let's stay focused on the low-hanging fruit, the items that cost the least and save you the most time.

Importantly, just as Simon helped Andre, you must understand where all your time is going.

I could ask you, or I could make you *show* me with your calendar. The calendar is better because it's not subjective and it's not open to interpretation. Simply put:

| **Your calendar can't lie.** |

The Meeting I Never Had

During our weekly one-on-one, my employee Miranda, a star-performer employee at SaaS Academy, admitted she felt overwhelmed after a recent promotion to team leader. She went from specialist to managing more people than anyone else in our company. "I'm supposed to review every employee on my team, manage their calls, conduct one-on-ones, and update reports. My head's spinning," she told me during a one-on-one.

Then she admitted that she felt like she was "letting the team down." I offered a Kleenex, some compassion, and a plan. I told her the same thing I tell all my coaching clients. That if we could <u>audit</u> her time and find what tasks were sucking all her time and energy, we could then <u>transfer</u> those tasks to someone else. That would help her <u>fill</u> her time with what was most important to her role.

Specifically, I told Miranda to audit her time by writing down what she was doing every fifteen minutes, every day, for the next two weeks. Then I gave her a few other instructions, and we agreed to touch base again after she did that study of her time. But four days later she sent this text:

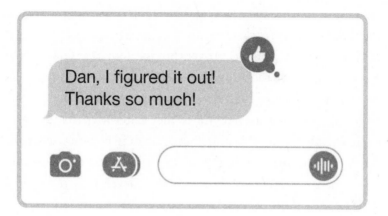

In just four days, Miranda was able to see exactly what low-value tasks were sucking her time and energy. To be honest, I don't even know how she handled those tasks—I assume she delegated them to someone else on her team!

I wasn't surprised when this helped Miranda, simply because I'd seen this exact tactic help dozens of entrepreneurs. She recognized what was sucking her into Delegation. Then she immediately eliminated those tasks.

The time audit I asked Miranda to do is similar to the same one I make every one of my coaching clients do—from the solopreneur to the multimillionaire serial entrepreneurs. It's a fourteen-day collection of every fifteen-minute interval of their day.

It's always fascinating to me to watch entrepreneurs worth millions compare how much they're worth to what they're spending their time on. I've seen business leaders worth billions who spend upward of twenty hours a week on tasks that they could have outsourced for *one-tenth* of what they're worth! They could easily have overpaid two or three staff members to do their work, but for some reason they never really saw it clearly.

But like the right arrow in the FedEx logo, once you see it, you can't unsee it. Once you clearly see where you're spending your time, you'll want to buy it back, trust me.

Some, like Miranda, never get through fourteen days without self-adjusting along the way. They start to see some really low-value items that are sucking their time (like browsing YouTube!), and after writing that down several times, they gain the clarity they need to fix their behavior. But more importantly, when they scope out the day, they recognize that there isn't just a pattern to how they spend their time, but to how their energy levels look throughout the day.

Time Versus Energy

People tend to work differently throughout the day—sometimes, in the morning, you can get through a huge financial report in thirty minutes. Later in that day, that same report may take you hours. Some people notice that after lunch they have another energy spike that, when focused, results in massive productivity. Others notice the opposite— that lunch causes a slowdown. Regardless, a time study helps acknowledge this small energy fluctuation so that later you can plan your week around your energy. (We'll talk about this more in chapter 8, when we discuss the Perfect Week.)

Time audits aren't anything new. I call mine a Time and Energy Audit because not only will it help you find out where your time is going, it will also help you see where your energy is going.

My friend Dana has been making roughly $2,500 per hour for years as the CEO of the Derricks Group. But still, he wasn't listening to my advice about the Buyback Principle. For one, I told him to hire an administrative assistant and stop checking his email (something we'll dive into in chapter 6). Dana just couldn't do it. "The argument was logical, but my refusal to let go of email wasn't," he said.

Do you know what finally got him to transfer his inbox? He started thinking about the energy related to each task. *Does this task (email) stress me out more than other tasks?* When he asked himself that question, the game changed from saving his time and money to saving his energy. He stopped checking his own email, hired an assistant, and went so far as to delete all his email applications on his smartphone. He literally can't check his email, even if he wanted to.

The 4 Steps of a Time and Energy Audit

I'll say it again: *your calendar can't lie.*

Once you've done your Time and Energy Audit, you'll know where your time is going.

Here's how it works:

1. **Determine your Buyback Rate.** You've probably already done this. Remember, your Buyback Rate is how much your company pays you, divided by two thousand, then divided by four.
2. **Audit every fifteen minutes of your workday for two weeks.** Using a piece of paper or an online template,* document every quarter hour of your time. It will look something like this:

   8:00–8:30 *Emailed clients.*

   8:30–9:30 *Conducted a podcast interview.*

   9:30–11:00 *Met with Board of Directors.*

   11:00–11:15 *Had a one-on-one with Kelsey.*

   11:15–11:30 *Had a one-on-one with Zack.*

   Two full weeks is the optimal amount of time for an entrepreneur to document so that one-off travel plans or interruptions don't throw off your audit.

---

*BuyBackYourTime.com/Resources

3. **Assign dollar amounts to each task using one to four dollar signs.** At the end of your time audit, go back to your list and write down one to four dollar signs next to each task. Think Google's restaurant pricing ranges, where each added dollar sign signals an increase in price. This will be specific to your situation. For example, you may determine that one dollar sign for you will be everything that's a $10-per-hour task, while four dollar signs denote tasks worth over $500 per hour.

4. **Highlight everything red or green.** Once you've collected a two-week swath of data and marked everything with one to four dollar signs, grab those two highlighters. (I like to use one red one and one green one.) Then you mark everything you love doing—everything that gives you energy—with a green highlighter, and mark everything that sucked your energy—everything that made you want to procrastinate or made you feel anxious—with the red highlighter.

After you've completed the Time and Energy Audit, every item on your list should have two components—one to four dollar signs, and either red or green highlighting.*

Here's where it gets really cool. Once you've finished assigning dollar signs and highlight colors, the Time and Energy Audit allows you to visualize your activities as if they were charted on the DRIP Matrix.

I love this method, because with your Time and Energy Audit, you've created a prioritized hit list for all the work that is draining you, starting with the Delegation Quadrant.

---

*Note: Some tasks may neither drain you nor light you up. You can ignore these. The goal for now is to clarify which tasks are bringing you immense energy versus those that are drastically dragging you down.

Time and Energy Audit

TASK	VALUE
Drive to the office	$
Make coffee	$
Check Emails	$
Team Meeting (Daily Stand-Up)	$$
Client Presentation	$$$
Run to the Post Office	$
Check Email	$
Sales Call	$$$$
Meet with Accountant	$$$
Quarterly Budget Review	$$$$
Employee Coaching	$$$
Check Email	$

GREEN   RED

Tasks on a Time and Energy Audit should include two components: (1) Whether the task is taking or giving energy, and (2) How much money the task is worth. I use red and green to show negative and positive energy flow. Then I use one to four dollar signs to indicate the monetary value of a task.

Making Smart Trades

Here's how you start getting tasks off your plate:

Delete unnecessary work. First, if there's any work that you can delete, delete it. Is there any work that is unnecessary? Sometimes we don't realize we're redoing work or simply creating extra steps. Often, once you write down these tasks, you'll see redundancies that can be easily eliminated.

Use current team members. If you can't delete a task, you want to delegate it. Can someone on your current team do this work? Too often, founders take on work that someone else on their team is already supposed to do or can easily perform. In those cases, just delegate the work.

Find a creative solution. If you don't have anyone on your team to take your lowest-value red work, then use your Buyback Rate to find someone else who can do the work. Remember, start with the lowest-hanging fruit. Also remember, it's possible to get work done for free—Martin and Keith (from chapter 1) both did it, and so can you. Just be creative. Use employees if you have them. Pay someone overtime if you can. Find a freelancer, a virtual assistant, or your nephew.

*

THIS IS HOW you start scoring quick wins, fast. Later, we'll talk about how to get rid of larger, more complex tasks. For now, attack tasks in your Delegation Quadrant.

A huge realization will come when you recognize all the tasks that are soaking up your time and sucking you into Delegation. If you can outsource those for your Buyback Rate or less, you can immediately begin trading like a true entrepreneur.

Some people scoff at paying someone else to do work they hate. I think it's selfish *not* to.

Let's say your Buyback Rate is $100 an hour, and you're spending twenty draining hours a week onboarding new clients for the thousandth time. Yet, you could pay someone else who enjoys onboarding less than $100 an hour to do that work while you spend your time on sales calls or something more valuable. If you *don't* make that trade, you're robbing someone of an energy-giving, money-producing job. Instead, once you transfer those onboarding calls and fill your time with higher-value work, you're then able to make more money, which would eventually allow you hire to someone else.

*

SOMEONE ONCE SAID, "The secret of getting started is breaking your complex, overwhelming tasks into small, manageable tasks, and then starting on the first one." Getting back to what lights you up and makes you money can seem like a pie-in-the-sky wish. But it's not.

The first thing you do is break down your life into quadrants. From there, you attack the low-hanging fruit, the quick wins that easily unlock exponential rewards (in both time and money). You do that by doing a Time and Energy Audit. Now you can start to see what's been robbing you. Use your creative mind to get rid of it. Remember, you have a Buyback Rate. Now you get to use it.

Getting rid of the low-value tasks sucking your energy is your first step into upgrading how you trade, into becoming a true entrepreneur.

Now, even if you've eliminated everything in your Delegation Quadrant, you still have another quadrant that you want to handle: the Replacement Quadrant. We'll tackle that in the next chapter.

5 Buyback Rules

1. A Level 1 trader is an <u>employee</u> trading their time for more money.

2. A Level 2 trader is an <u>entrepreneur</u> trading their money for more time.

3. A Level 3 trader is an <u>empire-builder</u> trading their money for more money.

4. $100 million companies weren't built on $10 tasks.

5. These are the only three trades you can make. Most people, even if they own their own business, are firmly entrenched in being an employee who is selling their time for money. Buying back your time starts when you begin using the money you have to repurchase your time.

Three Levels of Trade

Step into the Arena

If you want to upgrade your trading style, the quickest thing you can do is eliminate tasks in the Delegation Quadrant. Your homework for this chapter is fairly simple:

Do a Time and Energy Audit.

You can flip back through this chapter if you need a reminder on how it works. I have a template you can download at BuyBackYourTime .com/Resources.

CHAPTER 5

The Replacement Ladder

*If your business depends on you, you don't own
a business—you have a job. And it's the worst job
in the world because you're working for a lunatic!*
—MICHAEL E. GERBER[1]

WE MENTIONED ANDY WARHOL BRIEFLY in chapter 1. You are probably familiar with his famous Campbell soup pictures, Marilyn Monroe prints, and unique public persona. Most people know something about Warhol, even if only superficially. According to *The New Yorker*, "Andy Warhol's life may be better documented than that of any other artist in the history of the world."[2]

In the end, eighty-five thousand pieces of art as well as five hundred films have Warhol's name attached to them. In 2014, Warhol's artwork accounted for about 15 percent of the entire world's art trade.[3] Think about that: out of all art traded in the entire world, about one-sixth of the money was paid for work that came from one name.

Well, maybe one *name*, but not one *man*.

Perhaps Warhol's truest art was as a businessman. He found a way to continually reproduce his own ideas. He developed a cult following around his own brand, inviting people to his aptly named studio, the Factory. Here, he went from artistic businessperson to leading an empire. He developed his own method of putting photographs through a silk screen, letting the ink drip through, creating a very "produced" feel for the final product. He wanted to create art that had what he called "an assembly-line effect."[4]

And with his cult following, assistants, and fine-tuned process, he did, in fact, create his own assembly line. Not just in the way his artwork felt, but in reality: other people did much of the work for his art. Here's what the Guggenheim wrote about him:

The medium of silkscreen, which he began to employ in 1962, enabled Warhol and his studio assistants to create a prodigious amount of painting and sculpture in a fashion that simulated a factory assembly line. Through this mechanized means of production Warhol capsized existing notions of authenticity and the value of the artist's hand.

He used studio assistants, for one. For another, he borrowed from other artwork: he used many pictures that were already in the public domain—and therefore ineligible for copyright—and reproduced his silkscreens and then resold those. He also used others to write for him: he tape-recorded himself, then paid some young men to produce his book.

Warhol found a way to replace himself with others so that all his Factory's artwork truly was an "Andy Warhol" piece, but that doesn't mean he was the sole person working on it.

When you zoom in on Warhol's life, you'll see that he put just as much effort into his process as he put into individual pieces. This allowed him to eventually create on-demand, commercialized, reproducible pieces that he could sell for thousands. Here's one of his most famous quotes: "The reason I'm painting this way is [because] I want to be a machine."[5]

Warhol had managed to create a replicable process around what's arguably one of the hardest things to reproduce systematically—creative art. Again, he wasn't doing all the work himself. He was obsessed with commercialization, and, in turn, he commercialized art itself (something for which other artists have criticized him).

His lasting legacy is not that he has a few pieces of artwork that he hand-produced. It's that he built the machine that produced eighty-five thousand pieces of quality artwork scattered across the globe.[6, 7]

Andy Warhol didn't just turn art into a business.

His art *was* business.[8, 9, 10]

*

IT SEEMS ANDY WARHOL never got stuck in the Replacement Quadrant. He constantly stayed focused on what he was best at—commercializing art. Didn't have the originals to reproduce? Just take them from the public domain. When he needed to produce more artwork? Use assistants. When there wasn't the right process to reproduce artwork at the level he needed? Invent the process.

Warhol stayed focused on his Production Quadrant, but he *did* do something about all the work that needed to be done. He knew he needed processes, methods, and people to ensure all his time and energy remained focused on what he was best at. So he built a machine. As Elon Musk might say, he knew how to "build the machine that builds the machine."

When it comes to art—like sculpting, painting, drawing—it's easy to understand why people get upset about Andy Warhol—he didn't really create all of that art by himself. But in business, no one thinks that Eddie Bauer is hand-sewing every piece of leather onto jackets, or that Tommy Hilfiger is hand-stitching all the jackets with his name on them. While Warhol's methods were controversial in art, they're not in the business world. As an entrepreneur, you can take the principles and leave the controversy.

Replacing oneself as Andy Warhol did isn't that complicated. You simply need a path to getting there.

From Delegation to Replacement

In the last chapter, we talked about getting out of the Delegation Quadrant *fast*. Now I want you to know how to get out of Replacement and into Production.

I want you to find what makes you money *and* lights you up.

The Delegation Quadrant deals with quick wins—typically, simple tasks that can be outsourced to any number of people on your team or outside your company. Without much thought, or even a process, you can probably determine how to eliminate a majority of the tasks in that quadrant.

But the Replacement Quadrant is different. Here, there are high-value tasks that are important, and who you give them to matters. Warhol needed processes for his business, and you do, too.

Everyone understands hiring someone else to perform a task. I can't think of any leader who doesn't understand the concept. In fact, I'm not sure I can think of any three-year-old who's been told to pick up their toys who can't understand it: "Hey Mommy/Daddy. Can you please help me? I'll let you be my best friend." Effectively, that child just tried to hire someone.

Still, *billionaires* struggle, trying to figure out which tasks to hire out, who to hire, and how to efficiently manage everything. Conceptually, "hiring" isn't difficult to understand. It's the process we tend to misunderstand.

That's exactly why I developed the Replacement Ladder—a time-tested system for what business operations to transfer at each stage of your company. It works for every business, at any level, in any industry.

Here are the rungs, in order:

Rung 1: Administration

Rung 2: Delivery

Rung 3: Marketing

Rung 4: Sales

Rung 5: Leadership

Importantly, this isn't an *organization* chart, it's a path to follow, like stepping-stones. It shows you what to transfer next so that you can continue to buy back your time.

If I told you to "transfer all your responsibilities," you'd laugh. Likely, if it were that easy, you would have already done it. Some of them are important and cost a *lot* of money to give to someone else. Don't worry—you can follow this path, and, like Warhol, continually refocus your time on what you love to do and sequentially move up the ladder.

The Replacement Ladder

There are three key components at every rung of the Replacement Ladder:

- The *key hire* you need to make
- Your current *feeling* of stress or liberty
- The responsibilities that must be transferred to the key hire (I call this *ownership*)

Here's how it all looks when put together:

The Replacement Ladder

Hire	Feeling	Ownership
Leadership	Flow	Strategy & Outcomes
Sales	Freedom	Calls & Follow-up
Marketing	Friction	Campaigns & Traffic
Delivery	Stalled	Onboarding & Support
Admin	Stuck	Inbox & Calendar

Hiring according to the Replacement Ladder will help you avoid getting stuck in the Replacement Quadrant, as it gives you a systematic way to transfer tasks. At each rung, the entrepreneur identifies their current feeling, recruits or promotes a key hire, then transfers the ownership of those responsibilities to that key hire. Then the entrepreneur moves to the next rung.

KEY HIRE

The key hire is clearly critical. But get this: it's not the title that matters, it's the role. For instance, you could call the person responsible for Rung 4 a sales rep, head of sales, the chief sales officer, or a sales emperor. It doesn't matter. What's important is that that person is in charge of calls and follow-up.

OWNERSHIP

Maybe you already have dozens of people on staff, and maybe some of them are even technically in charge of some of the areas listed above.

Perhaps you have an administrative assistant, a sales team, or a marketer. Here's my question: do they have *ownership* of the right tasks?

Even if you have $2 million in revenue and fifty salespeople, until one person is ultimately responsible for the associated tasks of a given rung, *you* will ultimately own the outcomes. In that case, you can't move up. Until you can mentally relieve yourself of the responsibilities of a certain rung, you're frozen.

FEELING

Notice the progression on the chart from feeling *stuck* to eventually feeling *flow*: first you're feeling stuck, then you hire an assistant and transfer the responsibilities of calendar and inbox management onto them, and you start feeling better.

The feeling is particularly important if you already have multiple people on your team. Often, when I'm working with a sizable company, if I can figure out how the founder is *feeling*, we can determine where the company is truly at on the ladder. (If they say they're feeling stalled out, that's a good indication they're on Rung 2: Delivery.)

In any business I acquire, we climb up the ladder *in order*, starting at the bottom, regardless of the size or earnings of the company.

For example, I recently purchased a software automation company I'll call Outlandish Automation. The company already had twelve employees, but the CEO (also the entrepreneur) didn't have an administrative assistant. So I hired him one, taking him right up the ladder to Rung 2. There, we focused on delivery. If he'd already had this rung filled, we'd have gone right on up to the next rung, and so on.

If your company's just getting started, think about this ladder as you grow. If you already have dozens of employees, start at Rung 1, and go up the ladder. If you're having trouble determining where you're at on the ladder, just ask yourself: *How am I currently feeling?* Your answer's a pretty good indicator of where you're at on the ladder.

Lastly, remember: This is a matter of sequencing. Follow the steps in order, and you can climb the Eiffel Tower. Do them out of order, and you won't get anywhere.

And, I'll say it again. The purpose of the Buyback Principle isn't just to add one more person to your staff. It's to give you more time, at every rung of the ladder. Remember:

Don't hire to grow your business. Hire to buy back your time.

Rung 1: Admin

Key Hire: Admin Assistant*
Feeling: Stuck
Ownership: Inbox and Calendar

Without an effective administrative assistant, you're spending enormous time and energy on low-value administrative tasks. Your inbox is dictating your day, as you receive dozens of pings and you spend your time forwarding them to other departments, approving invoices, and replying to calendar requests.

As soon as you hire an administrative assistant responsible for the two tasks of inbox and calendar, you'll immediately begin feeling less stuck.

(We'll talk more specifically about this rung in the next chapter.)

---

*Also known as an administrative assistant or office manager.

Rung 2: Delivery

Key Hire: Head of Delivery
Feeling: Stalled
Ownership: Onboarding and Support

Some may call this rung "customer success," but the concept is the same. It's simply whatever you're promising to your customers. If you own a SaaS company, it's your platform. If you're a business coach, it's your business coaching. If you have a coffee shop, it's the mocha you're selling. Can you imagine Mark Zuckerberg still writing the code for Facebook (now Meta)?

For many entrepreneurs, their company's core product or service is emotionally difficult to outsource because they're good at it, and they enjoy aspects of it—Elon Musk enjoys engineering. Steve Jobs loved aspects of design. Walt Disney actually enjoyed voicing Mickey Mouse. If you own a restaurant, you may enjoy cooking. If you run a construction company, you may enjoy drawing up the plans. Warhol actually *did* enjoy much of his artwork.

In that case, I suggest following the 10-80-10 rule. You do the initial 10 percent, then put someone else in charge of executing on the middle 80 percent of the work, then you sail back in and finalize the last 10 percent, putting your magical touch on the project.

I doubt world-renowned photographer Anne Geddes, home designer Joanna Gaines, or composer John Williams are doing *all* their own work. Instead, they've effectively learned how to maximize their abilities by setting the compass for creative endeavors, then trusting others to carry the projects to fruition.

The 10-80-10 Rule

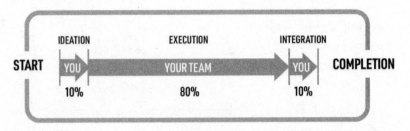

The 10-80-10 rule is a simple technique you can use when you still want to be involved with the end result, but you don't need to do all the work on your own. Think of designing the cake versus decorating it. Then, after the majority of the work is done, you come in to add a few special touches.

Rung 3: Marketing

Key Hire: Head of Marketing
Feeling: Friction
Ownership: Campaigns and Traffic

Does this sound familiar? In the first quarter, you drum up new business with referrals, creating new partnerships, posting content, upselling current clients, running ads, sponsoring events, or whatever you do to bring people into your café, your law firm, or your platform. You see all the new customers, the new contracts, and the new revenue. Then you drop the marketing ball to begin executing on all the new business.

By the third or fourth quarter, you've delivered on all that new business, but now there's little new business trickling in. So you make a plan to hit marketing hard again in the first quarter of the next year.

You repeat the cycle: quarter one, marketing. Quarters two and three, execution. Quarter four, business slows while you plan to do marketing next year.

I call this friction—entrepreneurs can *see* growth; they can almost *taste* it. But every year, they feel like an airplane that revs its engines and accelerates, but just before takeoff they lose speed, never getting more than a few feet off the ground.

A business will never grow—at least not exponentially—in such a manner.

Let go of marketing and put someone else in charge of ensuring that next month, next quarter, and next year there's still business coming in.

Note: Depending on how long you've been in business, you may already have a set of proven marketing tactics for ad campaigns, such as knowledge about whether ads, videos, or billboards drive more business. In chapter 7, we'll discuss how to transfer all that accumulated marketing knowledge to the person you hire by using the Camcorder Method inside Playbooks.

Rung 4: Sales

Key Hire: Sales Representative
Feeling: Freedom
Ownership: Calls and Follow-Up

At the fourth rung, someone's responsible for administration (administrative assistant), another person is onboarding customers and ensuring your product or service is delivered on time (head of customer service or delivery). Finally, a trustworthy person is executing a predictable marketing strategy that drives consistent growth (head of marketing). Finally, it's time to off-load the responsibility of sales.

I save this rung for second-to-last because you're probably the best salesperson, and you'll need the money you're driving to fund hiring for the first three rungs of the Replacement Ladder. So it's only practical to off-load this responsibility when it's necessary to continue growth.

Trust me—you won't *want* to off-load sales. Most salespeople simply won't be as good as you are. As the passionate founder, you can outsell anyone. I can pretty much guarantee you'll fire the first salesperson you hire because your expectations will be unrealistic.

Remember, *80% done by someone else is 100% freaking awesome.*

If someone else is able to hit about 80 percent of *your* sales capabilities, and you're reserving your energy for higher-level tasks, that's a win.

Plus, while entrepreneurs are *typically* the best salespeople, they aren't *always* the best salesperson even for their own company.

Once, I was handling twenty to twenty-five sales calls per week to keep growing my company. When I finally became frustrated enough with that workload (which took way too long), I hired Michael. I assumed I was a superior salesperson—why wouldn't I be? So I aimed pretty low. I figured Michael could manage half as many calls in twice the amount of time with one-third the close rate.

I had the numbers all backward.

He managed *more* calls, in *less* time, and *outsold* me.

Few salespeople will be that good. But that's okay. Don't shoot for perfection. Hire to off-load the responsibilities of sales calls and follow-up.

Rung 5: Leadership

Key Hires: All Levels of Leadership
Feeling: New Era of Production Called "Flow"
Collaboration: Strategy and Leadership

Notice the words *flow*, key *hires*, and *collaboration*. Once you get to the leadership rung, everything's just a tad different.

> **Flow:** Once you climb up the fifth rung, you can reach a level of freedom most entrepreneurs don't even know is possible. I call it Flow. Here, you become a Level 3 trader: an empire-builder.

> **Key Hires:** The number of people you need on your leadership team will vary depending on your business and

your industry. Often, a key hire from one of the other rungs of the ladder may be part of this team. Sometimes, they don't fit exactly. Regardless, at this level you're able to make the key leadership hires that run the enterprise without much involvement from you—a leader for marketing, delivery, sales, product development, et cetera.

Collaboration: This is where it gets *fun*. Here, you get to strategize with other people. You meet on a regular basis with your leadership, collaborating on ideas. They're running your business, hiring and firing, and putting out the fires. You're a bystander who has enormous input but little responsibility.

By Rung 5, other capable people are running your business. It makes money without your day-to-day involvement. You can continue to refocus your energy on your Production Quadrant because you've successfully replaced yourself in all the other areas. Yes, you'll still need to be involved with leadership. Frankly, I find that *most* entrepreneurs have this in their Production Quadrant—they love the ideation and creativity that comes from strategizing and leading.

Consider how you would feel if your current company afforded you the time to take a couple weeks completely off and still *grow*?

With a headspace free of the daily tasks of running your business, how many good ideas could you come up with?

With an executive team that can execute, how many of those ideas could you actually achieve?

Like I said, once you get to this rung, it's fun.

Simple Steps Add Up

You lose customers and their money when your business lacks organization. For instance, mom-and-pop restaurants are often superior to competing chains in terms of quality, but because they're inconsistent, customers often don't patronize them—the mom-and-pop café may run out of food, coffee beans, paper cups, even their customers' favorite desserts. And every time they do, they frustrate their core base of customers. The problem? The mom-and-pop restaurant owner is also usually the head chef, the chief marketing officer, the accountant, and the person in charge of counting the paper cups.

The minute the owner transfers some of the administrative tasks— like ordering—to an administrative assistant, customers notice that their favorite dessert is always in stock, and they begin to patronize more frequently. Similarly, with SaaS entrepreneurs, or other business owners, a simple increase in areas as small as quick replies, proactive check-ins, and on-time commitments can immediately increase sales.

Then the owner can move up the ladder to the next rung.

That's the beauty of the Replacement Ladder. You start with the economic resources you have, you identify the key hire you need to make, and then you transfer responsibilities to that key hire.

The Replacement Ladder is designed so that at each rung, you'll have an increase in revenue, affording you the next key hire. Eventually, you'll climb to the top of the Replacement Ladder where you'll be in the Production Quadrant.

Beating the Toughest Replacement

As I said, no one will ever be quite as good as you are at pleasing your customers. You've been at this for a while, and you're probably more passionate than anyone about the problem you're solving.

Programming languages happens to be one of those things that I know very well.

Once, I was giving my product development team a lot of feedback on a project. Naturally—because I knew a lot about programming languages and the issues my team was facing—I gave them some feedback on how I wanted the new tool programmed. Later, my head of product engineering, Raul, who rarely spoke, politely told me I needed to back off.

I'd told them *what* to do, but now I needed to let my team figure out *how* to do it—that was *their* responsibility.

I see this all the time with entrepreneurs—whatever you're great at is difficult to off-load. I was good at programming, so I wanted to jump in. But was it in my Production Quadrant? Not quite. I needed to back off and let my team handle it. Otherwise, I wasn't even following my own Buyback Principle.

When you crown someone else king or queen over a responsibility, you are abdicating your role, and that's why you feel freedom. No longer is it your responsibility. Jump back in, and you assume the stress, and you lose the freedom.

The Quadrants Can Change

Importantly, what makes sense for you to do today may not make sense for you to work on tomorrow.

When I first started my business, I sorted all the mail every Sunday, and I loved it. I enjoyed searching through the endless spam letters and advertisements for that one check from a client. Every time I found one, eighteen-year-old Dan felt like a real businessman as he skipped off to the bank to deposit it.

Several years later, sorting the mail was taking three hours every Sunday, and my Buyback Rate was one hundred times what it had been. Effectively, it was costing me thousands of dollars to sort my mail! Plus, by then I hated it—I had to stop spending time with my friends and family on the weekend to sit in my office alone for the afternoon. So I found an incredible lady named Lisa, who's been checking my mail since 2006. *Lisa crushes it.*

In another instance, my client Luke was having a hard time with his marketing lead. Every time his marketing lead got stuck, Luke rushed in with a solution. But someone eventually told him to stop and get out of the way.

Luke was having a hard time *particularly* because he was great at marketing, just like I was having a hard time stopping sorting my mail. At one point or another, those may have been life-giving tasks. At one point, my Buyback Rate may not have been high enough to pay someone else to do the mail. Luke's Production Quadrant may have realistically been marketing at one point. But a founder and their business can evolve. For both Luke and me, our values had changed, and our money had increased.

Getting Unstuck

In the first chapters, we went over your Buyback Rate and a Time and Energy Audit. These simple tools will help you eliminate time- and energy-sucking tasks that are pulling you into the Delegation Quadrant. Once you eliminate the lowest-value, highest-energy tasks—the ones that are mostly in the Delegation Quadrant—the real work begins.

You don't want to get stuck in the Replacement Quadrant, where you're making some money but not doing what makes you money *and* lights you up. In Replacement, tasks are meaningful and important. However, that doesn't mean they're the best use of your time. By using the Replacement Ladder, in order, you can scale up the ladder and out of Replacement and into Production. Remember the Buyback Loop at every rung:

> Audit where you're spending your time, energy, and resources. Do you *love* what you're doing? Is it making you lots of money? Check your feelings—how do you *feel* about your business right now? Freedom? Flow? Stuck? That's a good indication of where you're at on the Replacement Ladder.

> Transfer the tasks associated with that rung of the Replacement Ladder. Even if you *technically* have someone performing the work, if they aren't responsible for the rung's associated tasks, then you haven't fully climbed that rung yet.

Fill your new time with tasks that make you the most money and light you up. If you don't remember what those are, refer to your Time and Energy Audit from earlier: look for green tasks with lots of dollar signs.

You're likely thinking:

> *I want a solid example of working with an employee at one of these rungs.*
>
> *How do I make these key hires?*
>
> *How do I ensure, as Warhol did, that my processes will be followed?*

I'm stoked you're asking those questions—because that's what we'll be covering in the next few chapters.

5 Buyback Rules

1. After removing smaller items off their plate that are sucking them into the Delegation Quadrant, many entrepreneurs get stuck in the Replacement Quadrant. Here, tasks are valuable, but they are still draining the founder of energy.
2. To get out of the Replacement Quadrant, you can use the Replacement Ladder to systematically follow the rungs, in order, to remove tasks off your plate in a way that aligns with the money you have available.
3. Often, something you're good at (but isn't in your Production Quadrant) is the most difficult to transfer to someone else. You have some skill, and you *can* execute with a fair amount of expertise. But you can't move up the ladder until you off-load the responsibility of that task.
4. Typically, you'll want to follow the ladder up, in order, beginning with an administrative assistant. If you have an established

company with many employees already, it may be useful to consider how you're currently *feeling*, and then focus on that rung of the ladder.

5. There are five rungs to the Replacement Ladder, with associated *feelings*, *key hires*, and responsibility of *ownership*. Here's a snapshot:

The Replacement Ladder

Hire	Feeling	Ownership
Leadership	Flow	Strategy & Outcomes
Sales	Freedom	Calls & Follow-up
Marketing	Friction	Campaigns & Traffic
Delivery	Stalled	Onboarding & Support
Admin	Stuck	Inbox & Calendar

Hiring according to the Replacement Ladder will help you avoid getting stuck in the Replacement Quadrant, as it gives you a systematic way to transfer tasks. At each rung, the entrepreneur identifies their current feeling, recruits or promotes a key hire, then puts the burden of responsibility—the responsibilities—onto that key hire. Then the entrepreneur moves to the next rung.

Step into the Arena

For this chapter, I simply want you to determine where you're at on the Replacement Ladder. We'll get to how to hire later. For now, I just want you to get honest about where you're at. Consider how you feel, which employees you have, and the rung you want to get to next.

A. Ask yourself, *How am I feeling about my business?*

B. Then consider: *Which responsibilities of the Replacement Ladder am I currently struggling with, that are keeping me in the Replacement Quadrant?*

C. Finally, determine how you can begin to transfer those tasks to someone else. Do you need to hire someone, or do you need to simply move them off your shoulders and onto someone else on your team?

CHAPTER 6

Clone Yourself

IMAGINE HAVING AN OFFICE IN Times Square with a door leading directly to your office. You allow everyone to walk in at any time and hand you a to-do on a Post-it note:

> "We need to have a meeting this morning."
> "I need this invoice paid."
> "Please approve this campaign."
> "Where's your headshot?"
> "Are you coming to the conference in July?"
> "How do you want me to handle this financial report?"

This is how many entrepreneurs live their daily life. The moment they walk into their office, they take a deep breath, click on their email application, and dive headfirst into a sea of screaming requests just like these. They don't run their time, their inbox does.

While no entrepreneur would ever have an open-door policy to the world in the middle of Times Square, they do it every day with their email applications—they let anyone demand their attention, thus introducing distractions and sucking their energy. Essentially, they let their inbox become a public to-do list.

Why an Assistant Will Set You Free

Remember the Richard Branson ski trip in chapter 3? There was a secret detail that I hid in there—Branson's one employee who followed him on our journey. It was his administrative assistant, Hannah.

Halfway through our trip, I asked Hannah a question: "How exactly do you two work together?"

Hannah went on to tell me what she did for Branson (everything), how she did it (according to his system), and how he monitored her activities (syncing every morning at breakfast).

Everybody who screams and begs for Richard's attention gets a gentle "block and tackle" from Hannah. With her, Branson has no "got a second?" meetings and no "just real quick!" interruptions. Hannah manages Branson's life according to his rules, not the demands of others.

Some may call this position an administrative assistant, a personal assistant, an office manager, or a chief of staff, but the meaning is the same. From here on out, I call this an "administrative assistant." When used correctly, this position guards a company's most precious asset—the founder's time.

The truth is, if you want your days back, you *must* get an assistant. Maybe you already have one. Don't worry—this will be a quick chapter. Even if you *do* have one, you may want to keep reading, because most founders aren't using theirs correctly.

If you *don't* have an assistant, and your body tenses up when I mention hiring one, I get it. My coaching clients bring up nearly every imaginable excuse the moment I suggest they hire an assistant.

- *I don't have enough for them to do.*
- *I can't afford an administrative assistant.*
- *Why don't I just do the work myself?*
- *I want total control over my business.*
- *I don't have a system for them to follow.*

- *I worry other people may think I'm lazy.*
- *I don't feel like I'm busy enough to deserve one.*
- *How could I trust a stranger to manage my personal inbox?*
- *I'm nervous about having an assistant in all my personal affairs.*
- *It will take more work (and more time) to teach someone how to help me.*

I've heard 'em all.

Here's the truth: if you want to see your business explode, if you want to truly apply the Buyback Principle, hiring an assistant is non-negotiable. It's the first hire every entrepreneur should make. Every hour you spend on admin tasks, answering emails, managing your calendar, calling the gardener, paying bills, et cetera is an hour robbed from your business, family, and dream life.

1 | WEARING ALL THE HATS

When I suggest hiring an administrative assistant, entrepreneurs inevitably think, *But I don't have anything for them to do.*

For starters, return to your Time and Energy Audit from chapter 4 and look at everything you highlighted with a red highlighter that has only one or two dollar signs. If you haven't gotten rid of everything yet, ask yourself, *What from that list could I give to an administrative assistant?* There's a misconception that you can only give an employee one task:

"I need a salesperson for sales."

"I need a marketing person for marketing."

"I need an office manager to oversee administration."

You've been wearing multiple hats for a while now—why can't someone else? Remember, the goal is to hire for your time. Don't feel weird about passing off multiple tasks to the same person. The list of activities from chapter 4 that are sucking your time likely includes:

- Responding to emails
- Scheduling
- Project research
- Cleaning up data
- Updating reports
- Financial workflows
- Sending gifts to colleagues
- Travel arrangements
- Purchasing
- Administrative tasks
- Website updates
- Social media publishing

If *you're* still doing all of this, guess what?

You already have an assistant—you! You're doing the work of an excellent administrative assistant. My guess is, your Buyback Rate is a *lot* more than you could be paying someone else to do this work.

2 | BAGGAGE-FREE EXECUTION

Administrative assistants also have the benefit of executing without the mental and psychological hang-ups that make it difficult for you to execute. For instance, it's sometimes hard to bite the bullet and pay a huge invoice that you need to pay. Other times, you may not want to schedule the meeting that you know requires a tough conversation. But your administrative assistant doesn't have this emotional baggage. Think about cleaning out a home. It's always easier to clean out someone else's house than your own. You don't have emotional attachment to their junk the same way they do.

The easy way to know if something has personal emotional baggage for you is to ask yourself: *What do I procrastinate doing?*

Those tasks—and they may be different for every person—

can easily be off-loaded onto your administrative assistant. They simply don't have the same baggage you do. They just execute.

3 | GOING BY THE BOOK

Similar to executing without baggage, your administrative assistant will also follow rules better than you will. Why? Because founders *always* want to make an exception.

For instance, say that you have a rule that you don't accept projects less than $10,000 because you've done the math, and anything less than that will cost your company in the long run. That may be a great rule, but it only works if it's followed.

When a $6,000 project rolls through, you, the founder, will be so tempted to go ahead and take it on. You'll probably make excuses to yourself, or find a way to make it work. You'll accept the project, thinking you're doing a good deed, but then, later, you may start to feel resentment.

Your administrative assistant won't have that problem. They'll just respond politely, "I'm so sorry! We aren't a great fit for that. Here are some other options . . ."

It's just like the emotional baggage tied to certain tasks—you don't need to find out how to fight temptation, just use your administrative assistant to avoid it altogether.

4 | NO MORE BALL DROPPING

No one will guard your time like an administrative assistant will, keeping you on track and focused.

With an administrative assistant, they can reply to emails, send headshots, and otherwise ensure that the ball doesn't get dropped on projects.

Think about this: What if the next time you went on a two-week vacation, your company wasn't stalling while you were gone? Projects moved right along, seamlessly, as if you were there. Emails got routed correctly, and your inbox and your presence didn't become a bottleneck to moving forward.

That's a reality that a great administrative assistant can bring you!

The "Free Yourself" Jump Start

If you have an assistant, but you're still poring over emails, pay special attention to my brother Pierre's story.

Pierre, remember, was struggling in the home-building business. In fact, he was almost broke. Once he reconnected with everything in his Production Quadrant, what lights him up and makes him money, he got back to his real genius: sales. Within ten years (by 2017) he was killing it, doing even better than he thought possible. He actually found himself overwhelmed with all the additional work.

I suggested he hire an administrative assistant. But I didn't give him much of a *framework* for how to do it right. He hired an assistant, and a few months later I asked him about it. "I don't get what the big deal is," he said.

I couldn't believe that! My administrative assistant changed the game for me, buying me back *days* in my calendar. That's when it hit me: I hadn't told him *how* to collaborate with his assistant. "Pierre, does your assistant manage *all* your email and *all* your calendar?"

"No."

That's the problem.

Administrative assistants, at the minimum, should provide two support functions, as I outlined in the Replacement Ladder. First, they should systematically manage your calendar. Second, they should independently manage your inbox. Once I helped Pierre understand those two crucial responsibilities, the game changed for him.

If you already have an assistant and something's not clicking, make sure they're handling all your calendar, and all your email. That's the jump start you need to work well with your assistant.

Responsibility 1: Calendar

Your administrative assistant can do a list of things, but first and foremost, they are in charge of your calendar and email.

You should never be the first person touching either of these. You set up the guardrails and systems for how you want your administrative assistant to manage them, and then they perform. It's as simple as that.

In chapter 8, we'll discuss in detail how to create your Perfect Week so that every moment of your day is accounted for, but for now set some basic guidelines for your administrative assistant so they know when you'll be available for which tasks. Start with this:

1. When are you "at work," and when are you at home?
2. What time slots are you available for meetings (podcast interviews, sales calls, onboarding new clients, one-on-ones, etc.)?
3. What time slots are you working but strictly on deep, head-down work?

When someone asks me for a podcast interview, I route them to my administrative assistant. When an important meeting pops up, I don't know about it immediately unless it's *really* urgent. My administrative assistant doesn't need me to specify when to reschedule important meetings. They already know to schedule them on Tuesday or Thursday between 1 and 4 p.m. My assistant knows my calendar better than I do. I ask *them* when I need to put something unexpected on it. They take a look, and let me know the best time/day to put that item in— and that's the point.

I'm *not* in charge of my calendar. They are.

Responsibility 2: Inbox

The second thing your administrative assistant should manage? Your *inbox.*

If you're like most of the entrepreneurs I work with, you probably don't plan your day. Your inbox does. You don't decide what is most important to get done; the next email that pops up will tell you. Most entrepreneurs use their inbox as if it were a task management tool, in charge of reminding themselves about what's important, what's urgent, and what should be done next.

News flash: that inbox isn't your boss.

Just as your administrative assistant is in charge of your calendar, crown them king (or queen) over your inbox.

> **Make a rule for yourself:** *I am no longer ever, ever allowed to touch an email that wasn't first checked by my assistant.*

Can you imagine if someone else oversaw every simple, repetitive request on your time that's in your inbox? If every receipt, every request for a headshot or a meeting, every "quick question" email was answered *without* you, how would that make you feel?

I know what you're thinking: *I can't give over all that control.*

I get that—you want to make sure emails get routed correctly, clients are managed, and you don't miss important updates.

Don't think of putting an assistant in charge of your inbox as losing power, but rather think of it as gaining control of your time.

EMAIL GPS

To give up the keys to your inbox, you need a system that routes every email exactly as you want it to be routed so that issues are handled correctly and on time. I have a system called Email GPS that I, and dozens of my clients, use to maintain control while ensuring we never even need to look at most of our own email.

The Email GPS is a list of folders (or labels) that I've created that work for almost any entrepreneur in any industry. Armed with these guardrails, your administrative assistant can route 90 percent of your email exactly as you would have routed it anyway, but without you getting involved.

Below, I've listed off how the Email GPS works. Oh, and I know that exclamation point and the numbers look silly—but they're actually important. Many email services (such as Gmail) put your labels in alphabetical order, so if you keep the exclamation point and the numbers as you see them below, then your inbox will have your label (or folder) at the top.

Here are the specific labels in order of how they appear in my inbox:

! **Your Name:** Here, you'll find the few emails that only you can respond to: huge clients with big requests, one-off situations, and high-dollar decisions.
1. **To Respond:** Your assistant applies this label to everything they're going to manage but haven't gotten to yet.
2. **Review:** This label is for all those scenarios your assistant isn't sure about. My administrative assistant saves those items here, and every morning, we tackle these in about fifteen minutes: "Dan, I got an email from Emily. She wants you to speak at her conference. I think you should do it." I give the final thumbs-up (or thumbs-down).
3. **Responded:** When your assistant responds to an email, they put this label on it, giving you access to review it.
4. **Waiting On:** These are items that require action from others before they can move forward.
5. **Receipts/Financials:** This is for anything financial related.
6. **Newsletters:** Any content you want to consume goes here. Then you consume that content on your time, when *you* decide. Hint: Use an auto-sort feature for this.

To get the most out of the Email GPS, ensure that all your email is routed to *one* inbox. Once your assistant checks an email, they put it in

Email GPS System

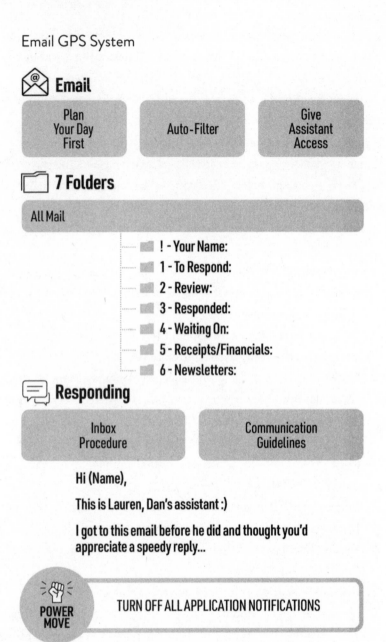

Email

| Plan Your Day First | Auto-Filter | Give Assistant Access |

7 Folders

All Mail

- ! - Your Name:
- 1 - To Respond:
- 2 - Review:
- 3 - Responded:
- 4 - Waiting On:
- 5 - Receipts/Financials:
- 6 - Newsletters:

Responding

| Inbox Procedure | Communication Guidelines |

Hi (Name),

This is Lauren, Dan's assistant :)

I got to this email before he did and thought you'd appreciate a speedy reply...

POWER MOVE   TURN OFF ALL APPLICATION NOTIFICATIONS

Many entrepreneurs don't want to transfer their inbox to someone else because they think they'll lose control. This system allows you to ensure emails are routed properly, without your involvement. As a bonus, once you instate this, you can turn off all your email applications, to regain focus.

the correct folder (or apply the right label) or archive the email. Consequently, your inbox should get processed so that there's nothing left in it. (In most email applications, you can archive something so that it no longer shows in the inbox, but it's still stored in case you need to look it up later.)

Using this system, my administrative assistant routes the majority of my emails without me reading them. They typically answer emails within a few hours. Clients and partners don't get upset that they're responding in my place because I've developed this simple email copy for them:

> This is Lauren, Dan's assistant:)
>
> I got to this email before he did, and I thought you'd appreciate the speediest reply . . .

Colleagues love this response, and the speedy reply they receive. If a conference organizer needs a headshot, for instance, waiting three days until I get around to it isn't ideal for anyone.

*

I ALREADY KNOW that a ton of the tasks from your Time and Energy Audit broke down into the two categories above—calendar and inbox. Simply put, if you can transfer these two categories of tasks into someone else's lane, so *they're* the ones managing them, your free time will explode.

The 9-Figure Assistant

While I was writing this book, my friend Jonathan was selling his company for nine figures. He called me and said, "Dan, I'm selling my company, and I like the deal. But I can't believe I'm going to lose my administrative assistant that I've built a relationship with for *nine years*."

I told Jonathan the simple truth—that he needed to negotiate to *keep* his assistant.

Jonathan had done a fantastic job for nearly a decade cultivating a relationship with his wonderful assistant. He had trained them well, they knew his family, and he trusted them. The last thing he wanted to do was start over with another assistant.

In his *New York Times* bestselling book *Never Eat Alone*, Keith Ferrazzi says it like this: "Don't think of them as 'secretaries' or 'assistants.' In fact, they are associates and lifelines."[1]

With my administrative assistant, I don't have to choose between urgent and important. Together, we can accomplish both.

*

I TOLD YOU that would be a quick chapter!

My hope is that you'll realize there is a path you can follow to ensure you replace yourself in your company in a manner that continually buys back your time so you can spend it where it matters most.

In case you're wondering, *How do I know those tasks will get done right?* Don't worry—that's exactly what we'll tackle in the next chapter.

5 Buyback Rules

1. An administrative assistant is the easiest way to begin transferring Delegation Quadrant tasks today. Every entrepreneur should have one. No exceptions. Even if you can't afford a full-time traditional assistant, determine your Buyback Rate and consider a virtual assistant.

2. An assistant can help execute on tasks because they don't execute with the same emotional baggage you do. Typically, they won't be scared to tell a customer "no" like you would be, because it's not really their company. Use that to your advantage by setting rules, then expecting your assistant to execute.

Email GPS System

✉ Email

Plan Your Day First	Auto-Filter	Give Assistant Access

🗁 7 Folders

All Mail

- ! - Your Name:
- 1 - To Respond:
- 2 - Review:
- 3 - Responded:
- 4 - Waiting On:
- 5 - Receipts/Financials:
- 6 - Newsletters:

💬 Responding

Inbox Procedure	Communication Guidelines

Hi (Name),

This is Lauren, Dan's assistant :)

I got to this email before he did and thought you'd appreciate a speedy reply...

POWER MOVE TURN OFF ALL APPLICATION NOTIFICATIONS

Many entrepreneurs don't want to transfer their inbox to someone else because they think they'll lose control. This system allows you to ensure emails are routed properly, without your involvement. As a bonus, once you instate this, you can turn off all your email applications, to regain focus.

3. An administrative assistant should be fully managing two responsibilities: your inbox and your calendar. You should never be the first person answering an email or scheduling a meeting (or anything else) on your calendar.

4. Founders wear multiple hats, particularly at the start of a company. Employees can do the same. Particularly with your administrative assistant, consider handing over multiple tasks.

5. Entrepreneurs often want to feel in control of their inbox, so they're scared of handing it over. Use the Email GPS system to hand over your inbox, while still feeling in control.

Step into the Arena

As quickly as possible, every founder should get an assistant and transfer at least their inbox and calendar responsibilities over to them.

If you currently have an assistant:

A. Ensure they're handling your inbox and calendar.

B. Tell them to set up the Email GPS system.

C. Hand over anything else that's in your Delegation Quadrant that you can.

If you do not have an assistant:

Hire one. This should be your next hire, regardless of what industry you're in, what size company, or how many other employees you have. Using your Buyback Rate, determine what you can afford. If necessary, consider hiring a virtual assistant. (For tips on how to hire, go to chapter 10.)

CHAPTER 7

Building Playbooks

Strategic thinking requires both diagnosis and design.
—RAY DALIO[1]

THE FOUNDER CHRONICLES THE RISE of the McDonald's corpora-
tion. Toward the beginning of the movie, Ray Kroc goes to visit the
first—and at the time, only—McDonald's restaurant.

Before he meets Mac and Dick McDonald, Kroc orders a ham-
burger, French fries, and a Coke. He pays, and before he has time to
leave the window, an employee hands him his bag. Confused, Kroc
says, "No, no, no, I just ordered." The cashier smiles and assures him
it's his food.

Kroc watches as an endless line of customers order food and,
within seconds, walk away with their orders. He can't figure out how
the restaurant is pumping out so much product (and revenue) in such
little time.

Eventually, he finds the answer: it's the McDonald brothers' Speedee
Service System.

They'd designed a kitchen to exacting specifications, then literally
choreographed the movements of all the employees inside that kitchen.
At one station, two people grill the burgers. Other employees apply

exactly five dots of mustard, five dots of ketchup, two pickles, and some onions. Another employee wraps the final product, and so on.

At each phase, a burger makes its way down the line and into the hands of another happy customer, hundreds and thousands of times a day. As Dick McDonald put it in the movie, "It's a symphony of efficiency—not [one] wasted motion."[2]

Kroc sees the genius behind the Speedee Service System. The genius isn't only in its ability to deliver a perfect burger within seconds. The true genius is that it can be *replicated* nearly anywhere on planet Earth. And that, as we know, is exactly what Ray Kroc did. He took the Speedee Service System and went big time, bigger than even the brothers had anticipated. He applied their methodology to thousands of McDonald's restaurants across the globe. The brothers started with one store in 1937. By 2020, there were almost *forty thousand* across the globe.[3]

McDonaldizing Your Life

In chapter 5, we talked about replacing yourself. Now we're going to talk about replicating your tried-and-true processes.

Every dominating company that masters scale—like Subway, Starbucks, and McDonald's—has exacting specifications of how they perform operations—in marketing, sales, delivery, everything. They have documented processes for every area, from accounting, to invoicing, to real estate purchases, to human resources. They'll tell their partners how to file an invoice, their employees how to clock out, and their executive team how to build a new location.

Most companies call these documents standard operating procedures, or SOPs. I call them Playbooks.

A Playbook is exactly what it sounds like: it tells everyone on your team how to execute a play. From how to run sales to how to open a new location overseas, Playbooks offer a way to transport knowledge based on what's already been tested and verified. "Do x, and y will happen."

If you know that marketing ads on Facebook will perform better than ads on Instagram, with a Playbook, your next marketer can start on Facebook. If your Playbook directs your sales team to follow up on Tuesdays because buyers are more likely to respond, the next sales team member can get up to speed faster. If your Playbook gives a detailed analysis on how to set up your credit card system, this can save enormous time and effort. The result, ultimately, is efficiency and predictability.

When applied to the company as a whole, Playbooks unlock scale. With the McDonald brothers' Playbook, Ray Kroc built an empire. He didn't need to reinvent the perfect system at each restaurant. He just needed to redeploy one process everywhere. Companies like Starbucks, Chipotle, and Microsoft continue to grow not because they're the best, but because they can execute predictably. They know that in the long run:

> **Unlimited predictability is more valuable than intermittent quality.**

Think about this:

- What if your next administrative assistant had an exact Playbook on how to reply to emails? Would you feel more excited to hire an assistant?
- What if you never again had to explain how to accomplish a mundane task to one of your employees because it was documented? Would you feel like you could accelerate throughout your day?
- What if your next marketing hire had an exact Playbook for everything in their department—from ad creation to generating marketing reports? Would you feel more excited to hire a marketer?

- What if your next salesperson had a sales Playbook, and in it they could find answers to questions like "When do I follow up with customers to cross-sell?" and "What CRM* do we use?" Would you feel relieved knowing you don't need to train them?

All of this comes from having established Playbooks. And here's some good news: You don't have to spend much time making one—partly because I have a Playbook on how *you* can create Playbooks. But more importantly, you can use a process that allows your *team* to create their own Playbooks.

Life Playbook 101

Playbooks can be created for anything, from simple tasks—like how to find and vet new leads or how to create company financial reports—to large Playbooks that contain all the information for an entire department. In other words, you may have one Playbook with *one* task, or you may have a Playbook with *multiple* tasks. We'll walk through both in this chapter.

The goal, of course, is to save you time and replicate a process without your involvement.

My friend Peter (a plumber) made a Playbook for billing because that's what was really causing problems for him. His company was growing so quickly that he was forgetting to invoice clients. After a few busy months, he needed to make payroll and buy some new equipment, and he realized his clients owed him thousands. Guess who was *really* upset when they got billed for four months' worth of work at once?

But Peter fixed the problem, easily. He made a video of himself on a Sunday doing all the billing. Armed with that training video, he

---

*Customer relationship management system, such as those offered by Salesforce.

now had a manual to show someone else *exactly* how he wanted the billing done. Peter now has a Playbook for the one repeatable area that was causing him the most pain—billing. Starting with the area that's causing *you* the most pain is a great place to start with your first Playbook.

Your Playbook system will grow over time. Peter could have a simple billing Playbook, or over time he could create a Playbook for everything related to financial management. For example, I have a financial management Playbook for SaaS Academy that's about eight pages long. It contains everything, from the financial reporting schedule to how to deal with clients if they missed a payment. If someone in financial management forgets what day quarterly reports are due, or they aren't sure which position is in charge of reviewing hours for part-timers, they can reference the Playbook. Although it's pretty detailed, it's not detailed to the screenshot level. It's written so that someone could go through it and feel mostly trained on all our financial management procedures without me having to get too involved.

I have a Playbook for every major area of my business—from how to hire, to sales, to marketing, and beyond. I even have a Playbook on creating new Playbooks!

I *don't* suggest starting there. I suggest starting with one Playbook in the very place you're having the most pain. That may be something as large as an entire department—like sales or marketing—or it could be as small as billing, as it was with Peter.

Regardless of the size of the issue, make your first Playbook for that concern.

- Are your salespeople failing to follow up, missing quotas, and leaving out important details for delivery?
- Does your brick-and-mortar team fail to open and close the building correctly?

- When the financial reports come in, will they be late, disorganized, and with the information displayed incorrectly?
- Is an entire engineering department disorganized, and no one knows when to execute or who's responsible for what?

My answer is the same: build a Playbook.

The 4 Cs of a Playbook

Here's my Playbook on Playbooks. First, there are four essential pieces:

1. The **Camcorder Method** (the training videos)
2. The **Course** (the steps involved in the process)
3. The **Cadence** (how often these tasks should be completed: monthly, weekly, daily, etc.)
4. The **Checklist** (the high-level items that must be completed every time)

The Playbook Framework

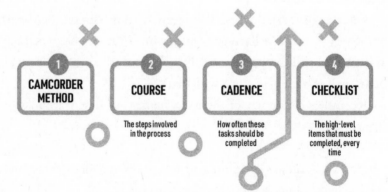

The Camcorder Method: 3 Training Videos for Every Task

The first tip I'm going to show you is how to build the training videos, the foundation of your entire Playbook. This Camcorder Method can be used to train for just about anything, as you'll see. Before I dive into how it works, I just *have* to tell you the story of how I developed this method.

By the time I was twenty-six, I was two years into running Spheric, with $1.6 million in revenue and twelve employees. I had no clue how to train, manage, or lead. I hired, crossed my fingers, and hoped. I opened an office in Bangor, Maine, so I could sponsor my work visas and cross the border to the United States (if you haven't figured it out already, I'm a proud Canadian) where most of my clients were. From my home in New Brunswick, Canada, it was about a one-hour flight to my US office, but I typically opted to drive the six and a half hours to force myself to train my staff . . . while driving.

A new recruit would sit in the passenger seat of my silver Volkswagen Jetta with a 2000s-era laptop in their lap and a power cord rigged into the cigarette lighter. I'd drive and talk, and they'd type.

This was 2006—a decade before it was possible to use your smartphone as a hot spot. To access the network, I'd placed a huge server in the trunk of my car, which weighed about fifty pounds and was as wide as a pizza box and a foot thick. From there, we'd run an Ethernet cable up to the laptop in the passenger seat.

While driving from one country to another, I'd explain the line-by-line instructions on how to operate the software program Spheric specialized in. Once, I even had two trainees in the car: one in the back seat watching, the other in the front seat learning to program while I drove and gave instructions.

After about half a dozen trips like that, I finally realized that I was doing the same training repeatedly. I realized that I could just film the training—once—and have every new employee watch it. So I did.

I now call this the Camcorder Method—and I just told you how the whole thing works. The only difference is, now I don't even record myself training. Like Peter the plumber, I just record myself doing the real task exactly as I want it done. Then I have my assistant drop the video into a Playbook. Later, I have the trainee watch the videos.

Think about a task that you wish you could delegate—payroll, opening your store on Saturday mornings, or filing that report—and then realize that you can train someone else to do it, without spending additional time training. Just record yourself. To date, this one time-saving trick is probably my clients' absolute favorite. Once I share it with them, a lightbulb goes off. Soon they've off-loaded numerous tasks (just like Peter).

Two quick tips about the Camcorder Method:

> **Talking is key.** Let's say you're logging into the back end of your website to upload a blog, and you want the headers, fonts, et cetera to all look a certain way. Just hit Record and get going. But make sure you *talk* while you're doing everything. If you explain what you're doing while you're doing it, it unlocks all the nuance you want captured.

> **Make three recordings.** Of course, every time you're performing a task, it changes just a little. Maybe you want to transfer the task of setting up social media campaigns on Facebook to someone else on your team. Well, every time you do it, it's probably just slightly different. I've found that *three* is the magic number. If you record yourself three times doing the same task, you'll have captured nearly every possible iteration.

I told my colleague Paul about the Camcorder Method, and he came back ecstatic after trying it just once. As an editor, he used to spend hours on simple tasks (like going over notes, changing dates and times, etc.) when he *wanted* to look for bigger issues in the books he was editing—like plot and structure. So he hired an assistant, used the Camcorder Method to explain how he wanted simple, repetitive tasks completed, and then he passed off those videos (without any additional training) to his new administrative assistant. To his surprise, not only did he save his time, but all the smaller things he wanted done were done *better*.

As you can see, the Camcorder Method lives as its own small hack, but here's how you use it *inside* Playbooks:

You put all the related videos inside one Playbook.

Again, a Playbook can be for one task or an entire department. If your first is a simple, one-task Playbook (like how to input customer information into the CRM), then those videos might be the only ones inside that Playbook. However, if you're creating a sales Playbook for an entire department, which you'll eventually want, you can put *all* sales-related videos inside that Playbook so that a salesperson can get all their training at once.

I love the Camcorder Method so much I now record almost everything I do on my laptop, just in case I ever decide I want someone else to do it.*

The Course: Document the High-Level Steps

The next part of a Playbook is the Course. (I know, I kind of fudged the wording here, but hey, I needed another "C"!)

Here, you create a bulleted list of all the high-level steps *for each task* in your Playbook. (Again, you *may* be creating a Playbook with only one task for now. Or you could be creating a Playbook for an entire department, role, or function, which will have multiple tasks within it.)

Let's say you're creating the steps for the task "opening the coffee shop." Here's how the steps may look:

---

*For more information on the Camcorder Method, go to BuyBackYourTime.com /Resources.

1. Clock in
2. Turn on espresso machine
3. Start the coffeepot
4. Write the coffee of the day on the chalkboard
5. Wait ten minutes
6. Turn on the "Open" sign

Notice how none of these steps are too detailed. They simply capture the high-level steps involved. Each task in your Playbook should have about this level of detail for each of the steps (again, you may have multiple tasks in your Playbook or just one).

One reason entrepreneurs fear making Playbooks is because they think it will take enormous time and energy. In the past, they may have tried to create an SOP with screen grabs, explicit instructions with detailed URLs, and directions on which software to use and when. After putting in all that effort, their business changed, the role changed, or the tools they prescribed changed, rendering the entire Playbook useless.

You don't need to create a Playbook as though the person using it is unintelligent. Instead, think of it as a list of what to walk through. What high-level information would you want to remind yourself to teach them if you were training them hands-on?

The Cadence: Record the Frequency

After you have all the training videos and the high-level steps for every task listed out, the next thing you need to do is create a section called "Cadence." (In a simple Playbook, this section may not be necessary.)

In this section, you create a list for *when* every task needs to be completed. Of course, some tasks don't have any frequency other than "every time."

The Checklist: List the Nonnegotiables

Checklists give you freedom. Books like *The Checklist Manifesto* and Sam Carpenter's *Work the System* have documented their power.

I witnessed it firsthand when my friend Francis invited my two young boys and me to ride in his small Cessna. I piled in with my sons, who were four and five years old at the time. We put on our little earmuffs and excitedly looked out the window. Francis fired up the engine and then pulled out a ring binder. We waited impatiently as he turned pages, checking knobs and lights. I was getting restless. But then he stopped.

"Hmm," Francis said, looking out the door. "Yup. Flat tire."

I looked at my two boys in the back seat, poking fun at each other's headsets. That checklist may very well have saved their lives.

That's the weight of a checklist. What could have been disastrous became nothing more than a simple fix, and we went another day. As *The Checklist Manifesto* points out, pilots and doctors have had checklists for decades, and they're nonnegotiable in their lines of work. I treat them the same way with my staff.

Inside each Playbook, I have nonnegotiable checklists. "Did you pull in all reports and ensure they were easily readable for recipients?" "Did you schedule a follow-up call with all missed contacts?" "Did you update the software?"

If something goes wrong with a sales report, a follow-up, or an update, and the checklist *was* followed, then I know the checklist needs to be updated. Then that issue never happens again.

*

IMPORTANTLY, A PLAYBOOK isn't going to capture everything, but it will save you time. Just like my rule with everything else—*80% done is 100% awesome*—a Playbook will ensure that 80 percent or more of a repeated process happens exactly like you want it to, giving you predictable results.

As a bonus, by keeping it in an editable document, you (or better yet, someone else who's responsible for this Playbook) will be able to update the Playbook as necessary.

*

LET'S WALK THROUGH two examples of a Playbook to illustrate how this would work.

Simple, One-Task Playbook

My good friend Mark runs a successful software company. In the 2010s, his company landed on a few awards magazines, and it started gaining recognition. Ironically, though, it wasn't able to grow because Mark was the only person hiring, and he couldn't hire fast enough and run the business at the same time.

Eventually, he took a camera, recorded himself talking about how he hired, then used those videos as the basis for his Playbook. Now he only does the final interview, and someone *else* does all the in-between vetting and preliminary interviews. Mark got back to doing what he does best—running an award-winning software company.

Here's how Mark may have broken down his Playbook with the 4 Cs:

1. Camcorder Method (training videos)
   - Mark records himself discussing how he hires someone.*
   - Then he could post that video at the top of a new document called "Hiring Playbook."

---

*Technically, the Camcorder Method would have meant he'd record himself hiring someone, but that would have been a bit awkward; so instead Mark talked through how he does it.

2. Course (high-level steps)
- Post need for applicants on social media.
- Post need for applicants on job boards.
- Review all résumés/CVs.
- Narrow list down to five.
- Send top five to interview with department manager.
- Send department manager's top choice to Mark for final interview.

3. Cadence (record the frequency)
- *The cadence doesn't really apply in this case: it's only one task, and each of these things will need to be done every time.*

4. Checklist
- Did we receive at least twenty résumés?
- Is each top applicant *excited* at the prospect of working here?
- Did you make notes to give Mark on why you love the final applicant?

That's a simple one-task Playbook. Eventually, Mark could combine this Playbook with other related Playbooks (like how to conduct one-on-ones, how to do a quarterly review, or how to fire an employee) all in one human resources Playbook. Notice that, in this case, the cadence didn't apply. In some cases, not every C is needed.

Now let's look at an example of a department-wide Playbook.

Large Playbook with Multiple Tasks

To make a Playbook for an entire department, area, or function of your business—like sales, marketing, or human resources—you follow a similar outline.

First, you record yourself (or someone else) performing each of the tasks that go in that function, and then drop the links to those videos inside your new Playbook. Next, you proceed to list the steps for each of those tasks, then put a cadence section in the Playbook that references when each of those tasks gets performed. Finally, you include a completion checklist.

Let's walk through an example of creating a financial management Playbook.

1. Camcorder Method (training videos *for each task*)
2. Course (high-level steps *for each task*)
   - *Task A: Get daily cash reports*
        i. Login to our reporting system
        ii. Pull report
        iii. Send to Dan

   - *Task B: Check credit card statements for fraud*
        i. (self-explanatory)

   - *Task C: Pay off line of credit*
        i. Check for line of credit
        ii. Pay off
        iii. If over $10,000, talk with Dan

3. Cadence (record the frequency)
   - *Daily:*
        i. Task A (get daily cash reports) must be done daily

   - *Monthly:*
        i. Task B (check credit card statements for fraud) must be done monthly
        ii. Task C (pay off line of credit) must be done monthly

4. Checklist
   - Did you pull all reports?
   - Did you forget any accounts?
   - Did you contact the right person for anything that seems out of place?

Obviously, I simplified this large Playbook. (Some Playbooks can be twenty pages long.) However, the concept remains. Just make sure the 4 Cs are in there, and you'll have a great jumping-off point. If you want a full template and/or more details, head to BuyBackYourTime .com/Resources.

＊

EVENTUALLY, YOU'LL PROBABLY want a Playbook for every major area of your business—from sales to marketing to human resources. There may also be unique things your industry or company does that you'll want a Playbook for. Trust me—Playbooks increase scale like nothing else, helping you clone yourself in various areas of your company without having to be involved directly.

But for now, go for a quick win. Find the one major area that's causing you pain and start there.

I promise that after you have one Playbook, and see your knowledge pay dividends in repetition, you'll be hooked, and you'll want another and another. Eventually, you'll have your *own* Playbook on making Playbooks!

If you're thinking that it sounds like a lot of work, you may be tempted to ask, "How does anyone find time to create all these Playbooks?"

Who said *you* should create them?

Why Make Your Own Playbook?

I actually use the Camcorder Method I taught you earlier to have someone *else* create Playbooks. Here's how you do it:

Pick that one task (or area) of your business that's driving you crazy. Record yourself using the Camcorder Method. Drop the links into a live document (such as Google Docs). Then tell *the person you want to transfer that task to*—perhaps a new hire or just someone else on your team—to watch all the videos, then create the Playbook themselves.*

Having someone else create the Playbook has multiple time-saving benefits:

You'll know whether they understand the process.
As Robert Kiyosaki said, "Teach, and you shall receive."[4]
By having someone else document the steps necessary to execute on an ad or how to open a new franchise, you'll know whether or not the other person truly understands your process.

Third-party documentation identifies missing steps.
Sometimes you just know how you do something. You've been selling your software to clients for years, so it all just makes sense in your head. You know when to send a follow-up, what questions your clients will likely have in the beginning, and what small little tidbits you can give them to be successful with your product. You "just know." And as you're recording videos with the Camcorder Method, you may have missed something. But once the *trainee* documents the workflow, then shows you the Playbook, you'll be able to easily identify the small, extra steps that slipped through the cracks. "I almost forgot—after we complete a project, I always have someone double-check if we've paid all our vendors." Having another individual repeat back what you've trained them to do makes identifying those holes far easier.

I record myself doing *everything*. From financial audits, to creating YouTube videos, to coaching calls with clients. Then I have my ad-

---

*The one thing you *will* need to help with is the Cadence—it may not be immediately clear how often you want each of these tasks done.

ministrative assistant upload those videos to a blank Playbook online. When it's time to transfer that task to someone else—often when I hire a new employee—I tell them to go through the Playbook, watch the videos, then create the Playbook.

Then I go over it with them to make sure (A) the Playbook is correct and (B) that they're trained correctly.

Bringing the Playbooks to Life

Training with the Playbooks is simple—have the new hire go through all the recordings. With a simple Playbook, there may be only three videos. Or, if you've collected all the tasks for a specific function or area of your business, you may have thirty or more videos. Either way, if it's within the role of your new hire, have them go through every video.

Then, have them read the entire Playbook if it already exists, or have them create it if it doesn't. Over time, these Playbooks will look quite extensive as you combine one task with another to create function-wide Playbooks. Even with that length, the incoming hire gets their feet wet right from the jump.

My final training trick is to ask them a few questions at the end, directly from the Playbook, just to ensure they read it.

As far as what tech to use, I highly suggest using a living document, like Google Docs, to create your Playbooks. If you want to make it *even easier* than all this, you can go check out Trainual.com, a company I've invested in that helps your whole team build out SOPs, onboarding, training, knowledge, and processes—all in one place.

Start with One

Just start with *one* Playbook for one area of your business, the one that will save you the most time and bring you the most reward.

Likely, you've already done almost all the work. Through trial and error, you probably already know which clients to pursue, what to look for in an ideal vendor, when to glad-hand your largest customers, and how to hire top talent for your organization. On all that effort, you're already getting some ROI—just like the McDonald brothers were with their one location. But when *Kroc* came in, he hit the copy button, and reaped exponential rewards on all the experience and knowledge that the McDonald brothers had already toiled to achieve.

Why not hit the copy button yourself?

5 Buyback Rules

1. The most successful companies execute consistency, not just one-off quality. If you want to scale your company, you must learn how to repeat excellence throughout the organization.

2. You can utilize the Camcorder Method to record *exactly* how you perform an operation while spending very little (if any) additional time. Simply record yourself (optimally, three times) performing a task. Remember to talk while you're recording. When it's time to transfer that task, have the trainee watch the videos.

3. A Playbook is a simple order of operations (sometimes called standard operating procedures). With a documented Playbook, you can hand off everything from a simple task to an entire department to help train the next employee and ensure they repeat actions how you want.

4. You don't need to make your own Playbooks. There are actually benefits to having someone else do it. To start making a Playbook, use the Camcorder Method to document tasks, then dump all those videos into a blank Google Doc (or other live document). Then, when it's time to transfer responsibilities to someone else, tell *them* to watch all the videos and create the Playbook. Check it at the end to ensure accuracy.

5. Every Playbook, once completed, should have 4 Cs: the Camcorder Method, the Course, the Cadence, the Checklist.

Step into the Arena

Your homework for this chapter is simple—think about that one task that you hate performing, and create a Playbook:

A. This next week, when you are performing that one dreaded task, record yourself. Optimally, record yourself three times. Then toss those videos—or have your assistant put those videos—into a new document titled "The ___ Playbook."

B. Then tell someone else to go watch those videos and create the Playbook.

C. Double-check the Playbook. Eighty percent (or more) of that whole Playbook should be done before you look at it.

Now you'll never have to perform that task again.

I have resources available for Playbooks, including examples, at BuyBackYourTime.com/Resources.

CHAPTER 8

Your Perfect Week

*Many of the opportunities you have in your life are generated
by the energy you create around you.*

—KEN ROBINSON AND LOU ARONICA[1]

SOMETIMES, I PLAY A LITTLE game with my coaching clients. It's a mini-test disguised as a simple question. I'll text one of them and ask if they have time for a quick call in the next hour.

It's a little trick, and it helps me gauge whether they're *reactively* meeting the demands of the world around them or if they're *proactively* routing demands into their calendar.

> **Reactive:** Without a planned day or week, reactive people will say, "Sure, Dan, I'll call you in a few." In that case, they're almost always just acting in the moment. They're just going to squeeze me in, which means they'll probably squeeze in a podcast interview, a client call, or anything else whenever it pops up. Not only does this mean they aren't planning their day or week, but in real situations (when I'm not testing them) it could put more stress on the other person. When someone tells them,

"Hey, we need to meet. What's your availability?" they'll be frantically looking at their calendar to come up with two to three chunks of time. Without any preplanned strategy on how to route meetings, they may just come back and say, "I don't know. What's *your* availability?" It can be a frustrating game of calendar chicken. It's like they're both saying, "I don't want to pick—you pick."

Proactive: When I ask to meet in the next hour, proactive people will usually say something like, "Well, I can meet on Thursday from 2:00 p.m. to 3:00 p.m., or I can meet next Monday from 1:00 to 2:00. Do either of those work for you?" The proactive person already has blocks in their calendar that work best for various activities— not just their time, but also their energy. They know exactly what part of their day is best for meetings, when they work out, and when they have family time. By politely offering me a few specific times, I know they have a preplanned week that they'll be able to take full advantage of.

A Jail Cell or a Peace Haven?

Can you imagine if a major commercial airport had a laissez-faire approach to when planes landed and took off? There would be utter chaos—passengers would never get to their destinations on time, gridlock would likely occur on the tarmac, and it would be nearly impossible to make connections.

By using highly specific time slots, airports move massive amounts of passengers every day. When unplanned problems arise—and they inevitably will—the airport is able to adjust based on an organized, preplanned structure.

While planning can't entirely avoid interruptions, it can help route them when they occur. By planning ahead of time, airports achieve an insanely high level of efficiency. In 2019, almost 80 percent of flights arrived on time. Commercial airlines may have upward of two hundred passengers per plane, plus there's a variety of uncontrollable issues—such as weather patterns and mechanical failures. Even with all of these issues, planning enables airports to make sure eight out of ten planes arrive within fifteen minutes of the scheduled arrival time.

Planning helps achieve a level of efficiency that simply can't occur with reactivity. Reactive people are also wasting a lot of energy and time throughout their day due to what I call the "buffer time" that falls between tasks. For instance, someone who's haphazardly planning events throughout their day could end up with a day that looks like this:

8:15–8:45 a.m.: Coaching call with Sarah, a direct report

Fifteen-minute gap

9:00–9:30: In-person meeting with potential high-value customer

Thirty-minute gap

10:00–11:00: Plan next quarter's ad campaign with head of marketing

Thirty-minute gap

11:30–12:45 p.m.: Coaching calls with other employees

Fifteen-minute gap

1:00–1:30: Zoom call to onboard new client

See all the gaps in there? There's a total of ninety minutes unaccounted for, and is anyone really getting anything productive done in fifteen- to thirty-minute time slots?

Ninety minutes lost every day by 1:30 p.m. adds up, but the bigger issue is the drain this puts on you—you're a founder, and you're able to produce at a high capacity. And when you create drag time like this, in the back of your mind you feel just a bit guilty, and that can weigh on you for the whole day.

Also, think about the energy lost. Coaching calls with employees demand one kind of headspace. In these meetings, you may need to be empathetic, soft-spoken, and leader oriented. You also may need certain tools, like a notebook, and you also probably need a specific environment—like an office space. On the other hand, sales calls require an entirely different mentality—you may need to "turn it on" with your personality, or you may need to bring certain presentations or statistics. Randomly rotating between the two throws you totally out of whack, ensuring you can never get "in the flow."

Every time you switch tasks, your brain has to switch focus. Some call this "context switching." According to a joint research project by Qatalog and Cornell University, every time a worker switches between software applications, it takes them almost ten minutes to get back to a high level of productivity. In another study, researchers noted that workers simply *felt* more productive when they didn't have to switch between their tools.

Context switching costs a few minutes here and a few minutes there. That's the immediate price. But throughout an entire day, if you're switching too often, you're never able to get into that deep state of thinking where your mind is focused, and ideas flow freely. Different theories exist about how long it takes to get into a "flow" state— some think it takes fifteen minutes, while others suggest it's closer to thirty. Regardless of the time, switching between tasks interrupts that flow.

Buffer time and context switching cost an entrepreneur a lot, but then there's what I call *bleed time.*

Every time I let a meeting run over or I get caught up talking to my friends at lunch for ninety minutes when I only planned an hour, I've created bleed time. A few minutes here and a few minutes there, and before I know it, I've lost one to two hours in my day.

The alternative is to take back control of your day, like my good friend Marcell.

Taking Full Control of Your Week

Marcell is a serial entrepreneur. He's one of those go-getters who's willing to put in the work. From his early twenties, he's been a tough, hardworking entrepreneur. His hard work paid off, and his company grew. All the while, he had a wonderful fiancée, and he was also a CrossFit coach. Balancing a growing business with relationships and CrossFit was starting to take its toll on him.

But Marcell is a typical type-A founder. He wanted to perform at a high level in every area of his life. His solution to get everything done was simple. He created a templatized weekly plan that allowed him to utilize every minute of his day effectively—a "Perfect Week" that allowed him to go from task to task in an order that accounted for his energy and time.

Typically, a Perfect Week does a few things:

> **Eliminates buffer time:** No more time in between tasks. Instead of having a thirty-minute gap in between meetings, with the Perfect Week, you stack those meetings on top of each other.

> **Optimizes for energy:** When you create a good working calendar for your week, you're able to see when your energy dips and when it rises, and at what times of the day you're most attuned to execute on certain tasks. A lot of entrepreneurs find that they're morning people—others, not so much. When you take control of your

own calendar and start putting tasks in around your energy, you'll find you get "in the flow" much easier.

Eliminates bleed time: When you plan your week, you are making it clear that there won't be bleed time, as in: "Whoops, we went over on that interview." Truthfully, there can't be bleed time. With a tightly stacked day without any buffer time, if you go over on one task, you're cutting into the time allotted for the next one.

Allows you to spot N.E.T. time: I've got to give a shout-out to Tony Robbins for this one! Robbins believes in No Extra Time—meaning, you can double up on certain tasks and "use time spent commuting, running errands, exercising or cleaning the house to feed your mind."[2] So while you're commuting or vacuuming, you can be listening to a podcast. While you're on an airplane, you can be reading. These moments allow you to grow personally and professionally while costing you no extra time. When you plan out your week, you can typically spot all those moments where N.E.T. time is available.

There is another benefit to creating your own Perfect Week, but I'll let my good friend Dale Beaumont explain that one....

The Secret of Task Batching

Dale is one of the top entrepreneurs in Australia. He was key in developing something called the Preloaded Year, which we'll talk about in chapter 14. He's big on batching—scheduling similar tasks back-to-back (Zoom calls with Zoom calls, meetings with meetings, podcast interviews with podcast interviews).

Dale is big on grouping activities because, in his words, "multitasking doesn't work." To prove his point, I invited him on stage at one of my in-person intensives in Boston. He first asked everyone in the room (several dozen high-performing entrepreneurs) to write down this simple sentence:

Multitasking doesn't work.

He timed them. It took the entire room about seven seconds to finish the task. Then he asked everyone to write down two sentences:

Multitasking doesn't work.

Now I really understand.

But this time, Dale put a spin on their assignment:

"Write down only the *first letter* of the first sentence," he said from the stage. "Then, write down the *first letter of the second sentence*. Then, write down the next letter in the first sentence, then, write down the next letter in the second sentence. Continue switching sentences after every letter."

Then he again started a timer. Immediately, the room was abuzz, as frustrated people kept trying to write *M*, then *N*, then *u*, then *o*.

After ninety seconds, only half the room was finished, but Dale put the rest of them out of their misery, telling them to put their pens down. He then offered the moral of his exercise. He explained that if one sentence took seven seconds to write, two should have taken about fourteen. But by bouncing *between* sentences, it took everyone at least *six times longer* than it should have, if they even finished at all.

That's why Dale believes in batching tasks—he's optimizing for flow. Simply put, when you batch similar tasks, you're able to capitalize on the fact that you're already in the right state of mind for that type of task. On a practical level, you're also in the right place, with the right set of programs and tools you'll need.

Using batching, here's how a proactive entrepreneur would plan their week:

They'd put *all* their sales calls on certain days and certain times, back-to-back. They'd do the same thing with their staff coaching calls, staff meetings, content creation, et cetera. They could easily grab all the right tools (iPad, notebook) and be in the right environment (office space, quiet room, or coffee shop) without having to switch between tools and locations inefficiently and randomly.

When possible, I take batching to another level, not just on a daily or weekly rhythm, but by planning *all* of one task on one day per month. For instance, I recently did fourteen podcast interviews in one day. This allowed me to prepare a few minutes beforehand, get in a quiet space with all the necessary tech, then proceed with one interview after another. When you batch similar tasks together, you're able to get in a flow state in which your mind focuses on similar information, and you're able to speed through with heightened productivity.

Here are some ways you could do this:

- The next time you need to approve an ad campaign, ask that *all* ad campaigns for the next quarter get sent to you at once.
- If you need to do weekly sales calls, plan to do them all, say, every Wednesday and Thursday afternoon.
- If you write a weekly blog, why not set aside one afternoon each month and write four or five posts.*

As a bonus, if there are particular tasks you hate doing but are highly necessary (probably in the Replacement Quadrant), you can put them all on certain days, knowing you won't need to deal with them outside of those times. I know some entrepreneurs who hate dealing with finances—by batching all finance-related tasks and confining them to one day, they free up their time and energy for the rest of the week or month, thus buying back their time for the high-value activities that they love.

---

*Of course, if any of these tasks are in your Delegation Quadrant, then maybe you can delegate them to someone else.

Perfect Week Example

	SUN	MON	TUE	WED	THU	FRI	SAT
6am				Focus Time			
7am							
8am				Gym & Coffee			
9am	Personal / Family Time		Focus Time			Focus Time	Hang out with Friends / Family
10am					Coaching Calls		
11am			Team Meetings			Team Meetings	
12pm							
1pm							
2pm		Sales Calls	Client Meetings	Client Meetings	Flex Time	Focus Time	
3pm							
4pm							
5pm				Day Close			
6pm							
7pm		Personal Time			Date Night	Personal Time	
8pm							
9pm				Wind Down			
10pm				Bedtime			
11pm							

Beware "Yes"; Respect "No"

I have a friend we'll call Rachel. She's a tough go-getter who owns a boutique retail store. She's also a mom and a wife and prioritizes fitness. She's been trying for months to do 75 Hard, an intense health reboot that requires you to diet, complete two forty-five-minute work-outs, read ten pages of nonfiction, take a progress photo, and drink a gallon of water . . . every single day for seventy-five days. If you miss a single day, you start over.

For Rachel to execute on that level with all her other responsibili-ties, she'd need to have a calendar and stick to it relentlessly. She strug-gles a bit, because she often finds herself getting distracted throughout the day. I've mentioned the Perfect Week to her because I want her to understand what she's saying "no" to every time she says "yes" to a dis-traction.

Rachel, I, you, and everyone else has the same twenty-four hours in a day. The problem is, when we don't account for all of our time, in black and white, on a calendar, it's easy to say "yes" to an impromptu meeting, an extra hang-out, or a last-minute errand.

When you design your week ahead of time, and account for all your time, you'll understand exactly what you must say "no" to in or-der to say "yes!" to something that comes up sporadically.

Believe me—I change plans when it's necessary. If I know my wife has had a rough day, or my kids need some extra dad time, I might make a sudden change in my calendar (or if Richard Branson calls and asks me to go skiing . . .). But by having it all planned out ahead of time, I know exactly what's getting sacrificed when I suddenly change plans.

Having your week planned doesn't mean you don't make changes—it just means you know what you're changing when things come up (and they will).

Adding Spice in Life

Sometimes when I talk about the Perfect Week, a creative soul begins to worry that their life is going to get too planned. They feel like all this is going to stifle their creative energy. I have a secret for you:

> When you plan, you have time for more
> spice, more fun, and far more creativity.

With the biggest events plugged in, you have guide rails. You get to make sure you don't miss the things you want most—like bike rides, time with kids, date night, and so on. The trick is to put *everything* into your Perfect Week.

Plus, when you do have extra time in your day, you can easily say yes to impromptu activities without guilt because you'll know all the important work is accounted for.

Bend Your Day to Do Your Best Work

In one of my coaching sessions, a cofounder client, Zacharias, asked me a simple question about where he should spend his time. As the technical cofounder in his company, he was responsible both for business development and technical development. Having his time and energy split between the two had him concerned about when to do either. "How do I split my time between business development and coding?" he asked.

"Plan to code whenever you write the best code," I said.

Okay, so maybe that wasn't the most helpful answer, but let me unpack what I mean.

While batching saves time, preplanning your week can also allow you to organize time slots around when you'll be most effective.

In chapter 4 I showed you how to complete a Time and Energy Audit. When you do one, you'll notice a pattern to how you feel throughout the day. Using this as a guide, you can plan a templatized week that revolves around your energy. (I'll show you exactly how to do this shortly.)

For instance:

- What if you had a few time slots dedicated to creativity *every day*?

- What if all your sales calls were scheduled only on certain days of the week so you could mentally prepare for them?
- How much energy and time could you buy back, simply by grouping similar tasks together?*

Before I had children, I did my most creative work late into the evening, and I planned for it. After my wife gave birth to two human alarm clocks (my two wild and fun boys), I've had to change my schedule around. Now I block off a few hours in the morning for my most creative work. Then, at lunchtime, I do a workout, which helps reset my energy and refocus. I do most of my face-to-face meetings, Zoom calls, and one-on-ones in the second half of my day. Again, most of these are batched to optimize.

By planning my week, I'm not answering emails during my creative time, and I'm not thinking about a podcast interview when I'm conducting my one-on-ones. Instead, I'm able to take the demands of others and route them on my calendar according to preplanned blocks.† This optimizes not just my time, but everyone else's. I produce better work creatively, I'm fully present during meetings, and any needed technological tools are more readily available. Plus, since I don't have thirty minutes of white space here and there, I'm getting far more done throughout the day, letting me come home earlier while feeling great about my productivity.

Dentists, lawyers, and professors have specific office hours, not just for efficiency, but because it allows them to be in a certain mode. They're more likely to give a better prognosis, come up with a better defense, or have a better explanation when their brain is in that zone. They plan their day proactively because it allows them to do what they do *best*.

---

* We'll go into the strategy of batching in further detail in chapter 14.
† Actually, my administrative assistant does this for me!

Engineer Your Perfect Week

Here's a few tips on creating your own Perfect Week:

Be willing to iterate. Having a preplanned weekly calendar is a must, but a Perfect Week is a bit of a misnomer—I don't anticipate that you'll nail this the first time around. Likely, it won't work well the first week or so, but if you iterate on it, it should only take about two or three weeks before you start seeing massive results. I still iterate on mine, even years later. The goal isn't to have the Perfect Week next week. The goal is to buy back some time and energy this week, then adjust, then keep on marching forward.

Honor your Perfect Week. Here's the downside to the Perfect Week: with no buffer time between tasks, your day will be very stacked. If you mess up, even by a little, your whole day can get thrown out of whack. If you let meetings run over, or you spend more time on a sales call than you planned for, you'll experience a cascading effect. So when you make a Perfect Week schedule, honor it.

It's about energy, not just time. The saved time is small potatoes compared with the energy saved. Business coach Michael Hyatt utilized a Perfect Week approach to help him stop dreading meetings. As an introvert, face-to-face time can drain him rapidly, distracting him from other valuable work. However, as the CEO of Thomas Nelson, meetings were also an integral part of his job. He finally set up his weekly schedule so that he only took meetings on certain days of the week.

He then informed his assistant that those days were the only times when meetings could occur. This allowed Hyatt to spend the other days in a clear headspace of creativity.

Important work goes first. As Covey once said, "The key is not to prioritize your schedule, but to schedule your priorities." When you design your week, put in the important tasks first. I'm talking about every important activity, whether professional or personal: workouts, meetings, time with your spouse, important project work. Put it all in. If you templatize a week without the most important people, dates, and events on your calendar, you're likely to achieve exactly what's on your calendar and nothing else. When you put everything in, you get another benefit of having a Perfect Week: you can also easily tell what you've been spending your time on—whether in your Delegation, Replacement, Investment, or Production quadrants. It's like having a Time and Energy Audit done ahead of time.

Then put in *everything* else. Put in all the tasks you need to perform, not just work-related activities. I include everything in my Perfect Week—lunch breaks, interviews, time for deep work, date night. By the end, my day looks stacked.

Batch work. Certain tasks require a certain headspace. Every time you switch between tasks, time drops in between. You can batch tasks into categories, enabling you to stay focused and avoiding changing location or environments. (Remember, batching can be especially helpful if you want to compartmentalize dreaded but necessary tasks that you can't off-load right now.)

*

RESEARCH SHOWS THAT small business owners (like everyone else) are wasting a lot of time—on average, about twenty-two hours a week.[3] They're performing tasks others could have done for them, escaping to social media, sitting in inefficient meetings, et cetera. The Perfect Week will help remove the time wasted that gets dropped between tasks. But ultimately I'm not just trying to save you thirty minutes a day from browsing your favorite YouTube channel. That won't kill you.

But here's what will kill you: a constant, nagging frustration of lost productivity.

Planning out your week, while a seemingly small task, will allow you to make space for the work you want and need to get done. Over time, you'll be buying back bits here and there, all of which can get redeposited into production.

5 Buyback Rules

1. You can be either reactive to the world around you or proactive. A reactive person is always available for anything. A proactive person has designated time slots to route demands on their time.
2. With a proactive, planned week, you will get far more done, and the most important tasks will always get done because they're *in the calendar.*
3. Your energy changes when you change tasks. A podcast interview requires one type of energy, while reviewing financial reports requires another. You can batch similar tasks on the same day to save time and energy by switching tasks as little as possible.

4. When you plan out your own Perfect Week, you can plan it around your energy, ensuring you'll do your best work.

5. When you plan your most important activities into your weekly calendar, you'll know what you must say "no" to in order to say "yes" to something new.

Step into the Arena

It's time to plan your Perfect Week. If you haven't done a Time and Energy Audit, I suggest returning to chapter 4 to complete that first. Once you're finished with that audit, head over to BuyBackYourTime.com /Resources to find the Perfect Week builder.

Remember to batch work and optimize for your energy (not just your time).

CHAPTER 9

The Only 4 Time Hacks You Need

I HAVE A CONFESSION to make:

I hate the word *hacks*.

I want to provide something that really works, and hacks rarely do. They overpromise and underdeliver.

But I've got to be honest—there *are* a few hacks that will change everything for you and your organization, giving you back more time than you thought possible. These four tools do not overpromise.

They are:

1. $50 Magic Pill
2. Sync Meetings with Repeat Agenda
3. A Definition of Done
4. The 1:3:1 Rule

Hack 1: $50 Magic Pill

When a professional tosses a bowling ball down a lane, it knocks over nine or ten pins. When my eight-year-old goes bowling, the ball goes straight into the gutter ... unless I put up the bumpers.

With the bumpers, he's almost as good as the pros.

That's what a few well-conceived rules do for your staff: they allow the inexperienced to flex their creative problem-solving minds without causing any real damage.

One of my rules, for instance, is that anyone on my team can spend up to $500 to fix a problem without getting permission. For the CEOs who run my companies, they can spend up to $5,000. (The other piece of the rule is, they must tell me about the expense at our next meeting.) Paul, the editor that I told you about before, has a similar rule for his administrative assistant, but it's only for up to $50.

The amount isn't important—it's the principle. Why get bogged down fixing a small problem when someone else on your team could fix it just as well without your involvement?

Whether it's $50 or $5,000, give everyone on your team an allowance that enables them to efficiently fix problems without ever having to get you involved.

Hack 2: Sync Meetings with Repeat Agenda

Remember the story about Branson and his assistant, Hannah?

The key part of his working with his assistant is their daily sync meeting. Every morning they meet for breakfast to go over the small percentage of meetings, emails, calendar invites, and other scenarios for which Hannah needs Branson's input. In less than an hour, he gives her all the direction she needs to execute any difficult one-offs. Over time, this list of one-offs has slimmed down significantly as she's learned to mimic his responses and decisions.

That's the level of expectation I have for my administrative assistant: that she can clone my responses to most situations without involving me. I want to keep every ball in the air, making sure all important projects move forward and decisions are made the way I would have made them.

I want all that, *and* I want my time back. A daily (or weekly) sync with your administrative assistant is the final key that unlocks that power.

Over time, my administrative assistant learns how and why I make decisions. As we build a relationship, I'm able to hand over more and more tasks to her because she knows how I operate.

I have a seven-point meeting agenda that creates the tailwind for all those goals. My administrative assistant and I walk through this agenda every time we sync, which for us is thirty minutes every other day. Over time, it builds consistency in her decision-making, autonomy in her actions, and trust in our relationship. It looks something like this:

1. **Off-load:** I keep my own separate list of to-dos, action items, and follow-ups. I update this list between my sync meetings. At the beginning of our sync meeting, I off-load all the items from this list to my administrative assistant, and she takes it from there.

2. **Calendar Review:** Next, we review my calendar for the next two weeks. We consider what needs to be added or removed, and we discuss where I need more or less time for tasks.

3. **Past Meetings:** My administrative assistant keeps a list of all my meetings since we last spoke, so during our sync she can review them, and I can tell her about any action items that came out of those meetings.

4. **My Action Items:** These are items I need to complete. Importantly, if there are supporting documents, emails, and messages, my administrative assistant provides all that information with the appropriate links in a live document.

5. **Feedback Loop on Projects:** My administrative assistant brings up projects that I've assigned to her so she can update me on progress, discuss roadblocks, and inform me once they've been completed. (Can you imagine never needing to ask yourself, *Did this get done?*)

6. **Emails:** In this section, my administrative assistant links all the emails she wants me to review, such as opportunities that have come in, correspondence she's unsure how to action on her own, and items that require my response.

7. **Questions for Dan:** If we finish all the above before our thirty minutes are up, my administrative assistant asks these questions to build context about me and ways she could better support me:

"Dan, how are you feeling right now?"

"How are you decompressing?"

"What recurring problems are keeping you up at night?"

Over time, my administrative assistant learns how and why I make decisions. The number of items in the "Emails" and "Questions for Dan" sections goes down, while those in the "Feedback Loop" increase.

The information lives in a live document my administrative assistant keeps. Between sync meetings, she constantly updates this document, including all necessary links. During our sync meeting, she drives the meeting according to this outline. Everything always gets covered. After years of crafting this sync meeting template, my administrative assistant recently said this: "Every possible item that could come up fits somewhere on this agenda."

This template also creates a fast on-ramping time for a new assistant. As I was writing this book, my main assistant moved on to a new opportunity and a new assistant came on board. With several companies, multiple direct reports, and a calendar crammed with meetings, it could have taken my new assistant weeks to get up to speed and be ready for the responsibilities I would lay on her. But with this template, after two weeks, she said she already felt like she had a good handle on everything.

Hack 3: Definition of Done

There's one thing many entrepreneurs think: *No one ever does it right.*
There's an easy hack to solve that problem: a Definition of Done (or,
as I like to call it, a DoD).*

I use this for every person at every level in my company.

For instance, when I ask my administrative assistant to purchase a
whiteboard, I give them a DoD:

> *This task is done when the whiteboard is hanging on the
> wall in my office, there are four colored markers (red,
> green, blue, and black), and there's a dry-erase marker
> handy.*

In simple cases like this, a quick, simple definition is all you need to
offer. In larger cases—say that you want a financial report ready—a
Definition of Done will need to have three things:

Facts: What are the hard metrics that must be accomplished? What measurement in your business must be
improved?

Feelings: How must you and others feel for this task to
be considered complete?

Functionality: When this task is finished, what must it
enable others to do?

So in the case of a financial report, if I were transferring that task to
someone else on my team, I might say that my DoD would mean:

It's submitted, by January 1. *Fact.*

I'm confident that the information is going to be accurate. *Feelings.*

---

*If you're in software development, you'll probably notice that I borrowed this idea
from the project management method SCRUM.

That everyone who will access it can easily pull out the data they need. *Functionality.*

See how helpful this is?

Of course, with the above DoD, the employee would probably say, "Who needs to access the report and what data do they need?" That's another great reason to use a DoD: it makes sure *you've* communicated everything you need to, and it forces possible delays to come up early, so you can keep things moving quickly.

So, next time you ask your staff to do something, don't forget to offer them a clear DoD. They'll be happier knowing what you want, and you'll get what you want.

As a bonus, after you've built a culture where offering this sort of instruction is normal, you can start to tell your employees to ensure they ask *you* for a DoD. That way, if you casually drop an instruction without much direction, your team can stop and say, "What's your DoD for this?"

Hack 4: The 1:3:1 Rule

This next one is called the 1:3:1 Rule, and I owe it to my friend Brad Pedersen, serial entrepreneur and cofounder of Pela, a sustainable consumer goods company creating "everyday products without everyday waste."[1]

Along his entrepreneurial journey, Brad grew tired of all the "upward delegation" he was experiencing—people bringing him, the CEO, their problems and dumping them in his lap. These problems were sucking his time and energy. While he wanted to focus on higher-level problems, little things kept creeping onto his plate.

To save his own brainpower for where it was most needed, Brad created the 1:3:1 Rule:

Before staff were allowed to ask for Brad's help, they had to verbally define a singular, narrow problem (not bring up dozens of tangential issues). Next, they had to consider and offer three realistic paths to overcoming that problem. Finally, they had to give Brad their single recommendation from the three options.

1 Define the *one* problem that needs to be solved.

3 Offer *three* viable solutions.

1 Make *one* suggestion from that list of possible solutions.

Brad was training his direct reports to think creatively and empowering them to make decisions on their own. In the simplest way possible, Brad was passing on one of the entrepreneur's greatest strengths—their problem-solving abilities.

Destroy the Ego

While most of these hacks will save you time, there is one thing you will have to sacrifice if you truly want more freedom and time: your ego. In many instances, these hacks eliminate an opportunity for you to jump in and solve a problem. If you use the $50 Magic Pill, someone else solved a problem without you. If you push for a direct report to utilize the 1:3:1 Rule, they have to come up with their own solution (even when you know the answer).

Nothing's more addicting than being the supergirl (or superguy) with all the answers. It feels downright intoxicating. But every time you solve a problem on your own, you're eliminating the chance for someone else to learn. All the while, they're growing more and more dependent on you for the answers. It may feel good, but over time one person has all the knowledge and expertise. Unintentionally, you'll have created a never-ending stream of upward delegation. At first, you can manage it; but if you keep up the pace, eventually everyone in the company will be pushing their problems upward, to you. Trust me, that's not a nightmare you want to live.

> You aren't the best person to solve *most*
> problems anyway. Remember, your work is
> someone else's play.

- If your marketing leader is coming to you with an ad campaign problem, aren't they more likely to understand social media than you?
- If your administrative assistant comes to you with a question about which organizational software to use, aren't they more likely to know which would be better?
- If your copywriter comes to you with a copywriting question, aren't they more likely to come up with the most creative copy-related decision?

You may excel at a few tasks. You may be great at a lot of them. But you're not the best at everything.

When you let go of the big "E," you gain four others:

Empowerment: Others begin to find the answers. More importantly, they begin to trust themselves to find the answers.

Exploration: When you require everyone to come to you with their possible solutions, creative thinking spreads like fire.

Equity distribution: When others bring their suggestions, they now have buy-in. If their recommendation fails, it's on them, not just on you.

Effective productivity: As you use these hacks with your direct reports, they'll use them with theirs. Everyone begins to be more productive.

If you want to live in production, you've got to hand over the reins of your ego.

There's no hack to that.

5 Buyback Rules

I don't love the word *hack*, but there are a few hacks that will save you immense time and energy:

1. **$50 Magic Pill:** Give everyone on your team an amount of money they can spend to fix problems *without* your involvement.
2. **Sync Meetings with Repeat Agenda:** The final hack to unlocking massive scale with your administrative assistant is to have regularly scheduled sync meetings. Follow the Sync Meeting template on page 151 to optimize the time.
3. **Definition of Done (or DoD):** Every time you transfer a task or responsibility, give your employee a DoD that puts you both on the same page about what "done" actually means. A DoD will typically include *facts*, *feelings*, and *functionality*.
4. **1:3:1 Rule:** (Thanks to Brad Pedersen for this one!) To avoid too much upward delegation in your company, require that every person who brings you a problem defines the one problem, offers three solutions, and then gives their one recommendation.
5. When you start using these time hacks, you'll need to give up one thing: your ego. Overall, as you off-load responsibility to others, you are telling them "You can handle this," removing yourself as the all-powerful savior of your company.

Step into the Arena

For the homework for this chapter, choose one hack and implement it this week:

- If you have an assistant (and you should!), implement regular sync meetings with a templatized agenda.
- Give every one of your direct reports an amount of money they can spend to solve problems, no questions asked ($50 Magic Pill).
- Offer a DoD to someone the next time you pass off a task (remember to include facts, feelings, and functionality!).
- The next time someone comes to you with a problem, politely ask them to come back after using the 1:3:1 Rule.

CHAPTER 10

The "Test-First" Hiring Method

A FEW YEARS AGO, I was in New York City enjoying a bowl of delicious, creamy, vegan ice cream. I could tell you about the flavor, the low calories, or the health benefits. But the real story is *who* I was sharing the ice cream with: Seth Godin.

Seth Godin is the marketing genius behind *The New York Times* bestsellers *Purple Cow* and *The Dip*. So when you get a chance to learn from someone of his intellectual caliber, you take mental notes.

I was sharing with him a few ideas on how I vet potential hires at Clarity. I told him that before Clarity, I'd had a fairly simple hiring strategy: check for pulse, ask for skills, negotiate a price.

By the time I was talking with Godin, I'd been thinking long and hard about my hiring strategy. He had great advice (of course), but nothing compared to this one nugget he dropped: "When it comes to hiring, I have one simple rule. I can't work with you until I work with you."

Seth Godin was pointing to a simple idea—why invest thousands into an employee without having any idea whether that employee will work out? Think of the other times in life when we consider making a sizable investment:

- Before we purchase a home, we do a walk-through and have an inspection.
- Before we get married, we go on dates.
- Before we buy a car, we test-drive it.

An employee who doesn't work out can cost hundreds of thousands of dollars just in their own training and paycheck. If an employee soaks up three months of time not providing value, you've given them a salary or hourly rate and invested resources into getting them up to speed. But all of that is pennies compared with what a really terrible employee can cost you. If you hire the wrong employee, they can drag down other top performers in your organization.

| "A" players like to work with other "A" players. |

Still, perhaps even *greater* than that loss is the potential impact on *clients*. I learned this one the hard way.

When I was running Spheric, I landed a dream project with Procter & Gamble (P&G). Not only would a reputable client such as P&G give me and my company more clout, but the project itself was ideal. P&G needed several new pieces of undeveloped technology. They would pay us to create that tech, and they gave us full control of the intellectual property (IP) to repackage and resell. A dream scenario.

I was in my early twenties, and I thought I needed a big gun to oversee the technical aspects. I brought on Chase—an older software developer with years more experience. I handed the project to him with little oversight. Four months later, I got a phone call from P&G:

"Dan, this guy's embarrassing you and your company. He's not following up, he's creating conflict, and we can't deal with him anymore."

After that call, we lost the job, the IP, and the client. Plus, I still had to pay out a huge salary to Chase as he left.

You're free to learn the lesson the hard way, as I did. Alternatively, you could follow a few basic principles that I've developed and tested. These guiding principles have allowed me to successfully hire (and keep) hundreds of employees over the years, helping me buy back even more time.

1 | BE CLEAR

Entrepreneurs often see the best in people. Plus, your mind is *always* looking to solve a problem in the most creative way possible. That means, regardless of what something looks like, an entrepreneur sees the solution they currently need. You've trained your mind to MacGyver any tool into the one you need to fix your present problem—everyone else sees sheet metal, you see art. Everyone else sees code, you see software. Everyone else sees a jumble of words, you see a book.

That MacGyver skill can work against you when you're interviewing potential candidates.

If you're currently in need of a world-class salesperson, what do you know? The next person you interview seems to be a world-class salesperson. (Even though they may have told you that they wanted to be a marketing leader. You didn't notice. You only noticed the line that said "sales experience" on their résumé.)

So, first, be *clear*, for yourself and your team, on what you're hiring for. The Replacement Ladder could be helpful here; just use the tasks in the ownership column. Even if you're hiring for a role outside the Replacement Ladder, you should be clear on what you're hiring for. Knowing exactly what you're looking for keeps you focused, enabling you to see past the other qualities that, while great, don't help you hire for the task at hand.

Simple, but helpful.

2 | CAST A WIDE NET

There's a reason larger high schools have more top players on their sports teams. It's the same reason the Olympics are fun to watch: The larger the selection, the more likely you'll find what you're looking for. To find a good fish, cast a wide net.

Sourcing a large pool of candidates requires heavy lifting, but there are few shortcuts. Below, I've outlined a few places to cast your "net." If you can afford to hire a recruiter part-time to help with some of the steps below, go for it. Otherwise, you'll need to block out the time for this process. Trust me, this is one of those instances in which investing the time is well worth it.

Existing Team: Your existing team should be your first go-to channel. Tell your top performers to go through their social media accounts and consider who they'd want to work with. As I said, an "A" team wants to work with other "A" players. Utilize that motivation and tap into their networks.

Job Banks: Some say that great candidates aren't looking for jobs. From experience, I know that's false. I've found incredible new hires who were waiting for a great opportunity. You can use technology to publish to dozens of job banks online simultaneously.

Admirable Companies: Sometimes, the best candidates *are* working elsewhere. Find companies you admire, those that have great training programs and great recruiting practices. Ask their staff, "Who's your favorite product manager?," "Who's the best sales manager?," or "Who's the best content writer you've worked with?" Keep a running list, and then reach out to them.

You may feel uncomfortable making these types of "cold calls," but trust me, everyone loves to feel needed, wanted, and sought out. Tap into that psychology, offer a bit of flattery, and then begin a relationship with almost anyone who may be a potential candidate.

Start slowly by just asking for advice on their area of expertise. This allows you to build a relationship that is centered around why you'd want to hire them and gives you a chance to get to know them and their thinking. Plus, asking for advice on a topic they're already employed in is a professionally appropriate way to cold-call someone. I use a simple "advice" pitch to galvanize relationships with people who are already employed:

Hey, Jennifer. It's Dan from SaaS Academy. Your team said you're the best sales manager around. I was wondering if you could give me five minutes of your time on how you'd build out our sales team. . . .

3 | GIVE THEM A CHANCE TO SHINE

Many entrepreneurs waste a lot of time on mediocre performers, when a simple earlier filter would have eliminated these candidates. The trick is to cast your net wide, but make sure the net has holes plenty large enough so all the wrong fish can easily swim away.

I have an easy tactic that quickly eliminates performers who wouldn't be a good fit. In fact, most of them don't even bother completing this, so it's a win-win: I don't waste their time, and they don't waste mine.

I ask every candidate to upload a three-minute (maximum) video of themselves answering five simple questions:

1. Why are you interested in this position?
2. What do you know about our company?
3. What is your ideal work environment?
4. What are your strengths?
5. Where do you see yourself in five years?

The video upload is important—this ensures that candidates can use basic technology. It's a hidden test embedded in the project itself. Second, I don't care *how* they answer the above questions. I'm more interested in how they think. Can they make decisions on open-ended questions? I value candidates who can think on their own, present confident decisions, and come up with creative answers.

4 | USE PROFILE ASSESSMENTS

There's a lot of science about personality and how that influences your job and how you work with others. Some people prefer to work alone, others are high collaborators, some people are great at finishing a project, and others are excellent creative thinkers in the beginning.

Knowing a candidate's personality to understand how they do their best work and how they work best with others is a key indicator of how successful they may be in your company. Importantly, I *do not* believe that a personality test is a sole indicator of how well someone will perform. It's a data point, something to consider in the mix.

Sometimes you want someone who has the same attributes as your other top performers on your team. Other times, you may want to hire *the opposite* (if you have a team of introverts, you may want to hire an extrovert). In other words, while I have every top candidate take a personality profile assessment before they're hired, I don't use that as an exclusive indicator of their performance. I treat it as one part of a complex individual.

Even before you start looking for any new candidates, I suggest running a profile assessment on your entire current team (if you have one). Typically, this will reveal some surprising results. You may find that all of your top performers have a certain attribute (say, an ability to deal well with stress). Or perhaps you'll discover that the people you enjoy working with the most have a strength that's a weakness of yours (maybe they're great at follow-through, and that's a weakness for you).

Then, use that test before you start hiring someone. That way, once you narrow the field down to about three candidates, pay for them to take a personality profile test. Most people love learning about themselves, so you can send the results to the candidates to keep for their own use.

I'm an adviser at SuccessFinder, and I think their methods are particularly useful (but hey, I might be a little biased). A few other popular personality tests are the Kolbe-A, the DISC test, and the Myers-Briggs.

You can try your hand at a few of them to see which ones give you the most revealing information. Here's a couple tips:

A. When you're hiring an assistant, consider hiring someone whose strengths cover your weaknesses. If your personality test reveals that you start things but don't finish them, you don't want your assistant to have those same flaws.

B. Don't turn it into a religion. You can use personality tests for every candidate, but people are unique individuals. People are surprising. Personality tests reveal a lot of information, but they don't account for everything.

C. Have your entire team take the test. It's amazing what you'll find when you ask your whole team to take a test, and then compare all the results! At SaaS Academy, I found that most of my teammates are exceptionally good at a few tasks, but then I also found that there were a few outliers who had opposing strengths, and that diversity seemed to complement everyone really well.

5 | THE "TEST-FIRST" HIRING METHOD

I opened this chapter with Seth Godin's simple rule:

"I can't work with you until I work with you."

Since our conversation, I've formalized his advice. Now I offer a test project to every single potential candidate. I call this my

"Test-First" Hiring Method. If you forget everything else, don't forget this part.

I've modified these test projects, depending on the role. However, the elements are all the same:

A. I give them a project that is representative of the *actual work we will do together*.

B. I always pay them.

C. I don't give many instructions.

My goal is to simply predict what our time together would be like. Will we work together well? Will we like each other? Will they save me time? Will they enjoy the work they're doing? Do they understand what this role requires?

If I'm hiring a graphic designer, I give them a graphic to design. If I'm hiring a writer, I ask them to mock up an article.

Occasionally, when I'm hiring a high-level executive or head of a department, I'll need to create a hypothetical scenario. So for a marketing lead role, I may suggest a real problem I've seen with our marketing ads, then ask them how they would increase our click-through rate. If I'm hiring a sales leader, I'd anonymize a previous real scenario and ask them how they'd coach one of their sales team members.

Here's an example of a real test project I've given to one of my assistants: "Send a thoughtful gift to Kyle at Proposify."

Notice that I don't give many instructions. I want to understand how my potential assistant uses resources and how independently they'll work. I'm allowing them to bring their own creativity, and I'm also teasing out whether this candidate will *save me time* by figuring things out on their own or *cost me time* by stalling and refusing to make their own decisions. I'm less concerned with them "nailing it." If they send me fourteen emails with questions, then we aren't a match. If they research Kyle, then send him a thoughtful gift, now I know this candidate has technical chops, creativity, and empathy—all must-haves for my team.

6 | SELL THE FUTURE

Most candidates filter themselves out at the video upload stage. Maybe three to five actually follow the instructions to the letter. By the time those few complete a test project, there's usually one stand-out individual.

At the beginning of the hiring process, candidates are selling themselves to me. Once I know who I want, I sell myself to *them*. Once I know who I want to hire (after the test project), my mindset switches over.

Like most good salespeople, you don't just sell what you have. You connect what you have with what the buyer wants. Salt can be used in a variety of ways: as a preservative, as a seasoning, even as a chemical. Similarly, your company has a lot to offer: promotional opportunities, a paycheck, friends, community, personal growth, professional growth, network enhancement, résumé building, and a lifelong career. If you want to sell the future, you need to find out what your top candidate *wants*, then ensure you're aligned in that endeavor.

Gary Vaynerchuk—you know, *the* Gary Vee, four-time *New York Times* bestselling author and leader of VaynerMedia—is a master at selling the future to his candidates. He starts by deeply listening to them during the interview stage, understanding what they desire, then connecting what he has to offer to those desires. It's not gamesmanship: Gary Vee knows that if he delivers on what top talent is striving for—whether it's title, prestige, opportunity, pay, or a new skill set—they'll work hard, provide value, and stay longer. Gary Vee says he spends *the entire interview* just trying to get an honest answer about what the employee wants. "I don't care what your agenda is, I just want to know what it is, so I can help us get there."[1]

Once Gary Vee finds out what an employee wants, regardless of what that is, he's able to execute on that.

Personally, I get superspecific on the candidate's desires. I usually ask something like, "Where do you want to be *in five years*?" This gives me a clear idea of whether I can help them achieve what they want with my current business. If they're after a certain title, does their potential role have upward mobility? If they're after a certain pay scale, what would it take to get them there? If they have other aspirational dreams, like living in a certain location or spending time with family, will this role help or hurt those dreams?

Once I find alignment with a top candidate, I sell, and I sell hard.

Hire Right, Save Time

If you want to save time, you hire the right person to buy that time back. They must be capable of managing the tasks on their own, using available resources. The goal isn't to fill a simple role: it's to move tasks off your plate and onto someone else's.

The time you'll save with the right person will be enormous, and they will more than pay for themselves. The wrong hire will cost you more time, energy, headache, and money than you can imagine.

With clarity on what you're looking for in your potential candidate, you can cast a wide net to catch many fish. With a few good filters, you can allow candidates to self-select out of your company. Finally, you must sell, and sell hard. Top talent is a game changer. Once you've put in the effort and found the diamond in the cave, mine it.

Of course, you must ensure they're equipped to conquer their role—and that's exactly what we'll cover in the next chapter.

6 Buyback Rules

This chapter, we've got *six* things to remember.

1. **Be clear:** Remember to be certain about what you're looking for in a candidate.
2. **Cast a wide net:** Hiring ultimately comes down to numbers. To get a large number of qualified candidates, ask current employees, use job boards, and look for those who are currently working.
3. **Require a video:** Ask all candidates to upload a three-minute video. Right here, many people who didn't read the instructions will self-eliminate.
4. **Use profile assessments:** Have each candidate (who's made it this far) do a personality assessment.
5. **The "Test-First" Hiring Method:** Don't work with someone until you've worked with them. Have your final few candidates perform a test task.
6. **Sell the future:** Once you've narrowed your list to the one right candidate, switch gears. Now you want to sell the role *to them*.

Step into the Arena

Some of the above work will take some time. But you can get a quick start with these two moves:

A. To hire correctly, the first thing you need to do is know *who* you're hiring and *why*. You can return to the Replacement Ladder to determine where you're at, if you need to. Next, take out a pen and paper and begin to draw out exactly which tasks this person would be responsible for. Remember, the goal is to always *save you time*.

B. Once you know the tasks and responsibilities you'd transfer onto that new hire, let everyone on your staff know you're hiring, and ask if they know of a qualified candidate who fits that description.

Now you're already halfway through Step 2 ("Cast a wide net") of hiring like Seth Godin.

CHAPTER 11

Transformational Leadership

*Don't tell people how to do things, tell them what to do
and let them surprise you with their results.*

—GENERAL GEORGE PATTON

ADAM, MY HEAD OF PEOPLE, came to me in 2021 with a problem.

"I need to hire eleven people in the next quarter. How on Earth am I going to do that?!"

Adam was feeling pressure. I checked to make sure he didn't just need someone to listen. He didn't. He wanted a solution. So I directed Adam to the hiring manager in his department: Adam.

"Adam, if you need help, I'll cancel meetings, brainstorm, do whatever's necessary to support you. However, ultimately, this is why I hired you," I told him. He got up, cracked a smile, and left the room.

"I'll be back after I've thought more about it."

But just like Miranda in chapter 4, he never came back. Two months later, we ended up with eleven outstanding new team members.

Other People's Monkeys

What I did with Adam was simple: I transferred the ownership of the solution back onto Adam.

In Ken Blanchard's book *The One Minute Manager Meets the Monkey*, Blanchard calls these types of situations "other people's monkeys." As a leader, you must ensure you aren't accidentally taking on other people's monkeys (problems or projects). Adam was (probably unintentionally) trying to put *his* monkey on *my* back. I gave the monkey a nice pat on the head and told him to go back home.

That's the basis of transformational leadership: start with the premise that this isn't your job, it's theirs. You shouldn't be telling them how to do it because it's their role, and they own it. Instead, they should be explaining to *you* the best way to solve it.

Transactional Management Versus Transformational Leadership

Nine out of ten entrepreneurs get trapped in the vicious circle of what I call transactional management: they *tell* people what to do, then *check* that they did it, then give them what to do *next*.

Here's what the daily routine looks like for a leader using transactional management:

When they get to the office, they examine employee number one, ensuring the employee did as they were told, checking their work, then telling them what to do next. If they're stuck, the leader helps get them unstuck.

Then the transactional leader meets with direct report number two for the same reasons—to ensure they did what they were last told, check their work, and tell them what to do next.

Rinse and repeat, going through every single direct report.

Every leader who goes through this cycle will end up hitting what I call the tell-check-next ceiling, at which point they simply can't handle any more work. I hit the tell-check-next ceiling after using this approach for two years at my first successful company, Spheric.

At twelve reports, I couldn't manage any more. But to keep up with growth, we needed to hire another developer, even though there was no way I could possibly manage one more person. Then I read *High Output Management* by Andy Grove. He helped me understand that to break through the tell-check-next ceiling, I had to lead differently. Using Grove's and others' lessons, I changed my beliefs and built a new plan. (While Grove calls this high output management, I call my version transformational leadership.)

Under transformational leadership, you replace tell-check-next with three other actions:

Transactional Management vs. Transformational Leadership

Transactional Management	Transformational Leadership
1 **Tell**	1 **Outcome**
2 **Check**	2 **Measure**
3 **Next**	3 **Coach**

The changes may seem semantic at first, but I assure you, the differences can save immense stress and time. Once *you* change the way you lead, leaders under you will change the way they lead. Overall, you can give your entire company a new way of thinking, one that empowers every employee to take responsibility over their role.

~~Tell~~ Outcome

It doesn't make sense to hire smart people and tell them what
to do; we hire smart people so they can tell us what to do.

—STEVE JOBS

With transformational leadership, you stop leading by telling someone *how* to do something and instead tell them *what* needs to get done. You set the outcomes, and you put the onus of responsibility on them.

In chapters 7 and 9, we talked about assigning outcomes, like email and calendar, or onboarding and support. Outcomes can be that broad, or they can be as small and simple as "run payroll for this week."

How would you feel if it wasn't your job to tell your salesperson how to sell the next client? Or your marketing leader how to create the next ad campaign? Or your customer success manager how to handle that customer complaint?

With transformational leadership, every time you give an instruction, you aren't telling others exactly how to do it, but what needs to get done. How? Well, that's up to them.

> "Bethany, please spell-check blog posts before they go out" becomes "Bethany, the blog posts must always be error free."

> "Danielle, all employees need to take a class on the new GDPR updates" becomes "Danielle, we must be GDPR compliant."

> "James, you need to make more sales calls" becomes "James, you need to hit one hundred thousand dollars in sales by the end of the quarter."

> "Maloney, increase the menu prices" becomes "Maloney, we need to make ten percent more per square foot in every brick-and-mortar location."

The changes may seem small, but notice the subtle shift in responsibility that comes with each changed statement. Before, the leader has taken on the mental stress of achieving an outcome, then tried to determine the best way to get there.

Studies have consistently shown that "decision fatigue" can set in after a leader—or anyone else—makes repeated decisions. In one study, researchers at universities in California looked at the decisions of financial analysts when it came to predicting how a company's stock would perform. They found that decisions made earlier in the day were more accurate than decisions made later in the day. Further, the analysts tended to simply rely on earlier decisions to compensate for their fatigue:

> *Forecast accuracy declines over the course of a day as the number of forecasts the analyst has already issued increases. Also consistent with decision fatigue, we find that the more forecasts an analyst issues, the higher the likelihood the analyst resorts to . . . reissuing their own previous outstanding forecasts.*[1]

In other words—we're all only going to make a limited number of excellent decisions today. Let's save those for the area where we can produce the most benefits (our Production Quadrant).

Once the outcomes were shifted to Bethany, Danielle, James, and Maloney, they could take on the mental responsibility and feel empowered to make the best decisions themselves. This subtle shift is important for four reasons:

1. Your employees are closer to the problem and may have more information than you do.
2. They have more time and energy to solve the problem and, as a result, more creativity.
3. By shifting responsibility, you're forcing them to increase their capabilities.

4. When the solution is theirs, they're more likely to be excited about it and champion that decision and ensure its implementation is completed.

Forcing employees to get creative and devise their own solutions often leads to increased efficiency and better outcomes. For example, Bethany, Danielle, James, and Maloney might've come up with the following:

	Transactional Management	Results	Transformational Leadership	Results
Bethany	"Bethany, please spell-check blog posts before they go out."	*Bethany edits every blog post, costing about fifteen staff-hours per week.	"Bethany, the blog posts must always be error free."	*Bethany researches and finds an inexpensive AI program that eliminates 90 percent of human errors automatically, reducing the needed staff-hours. *Bethany knows that a junior staff member under her wants to get into editing, so she gives them the opportunity to do the final edits, costing little in additional staff-hours and inspiring a new team member.
Danielle	"Danielle, the new employees need to take a class on the new GDPR updates."	*Danielle sends all employees to the GDPR class, costing the company thousands.	"Danielle, we must be GDPR compliant."	*Danielle researches the issue, and then decides that only she needs to take a GDPR certification. She gets certified, then creates a bullet point list of the ten most important items for everyone across the company. *No employees sit in a boring class.

	Transactional Management	Results	Transformational Leadership	Results
James	"James, you need to make more sales calls."	*James makes more sales calls.	"James, you need to hit one hundred thousand dollars in sales by the end of the quarter."	*James knows he's great at sales calls but lacks in follow-up and cross-selling. He asks his colleagues how they schedule follow-up calls and reads a book on cross-selling. *James increases his sales skills, which he can now use anywhere, even if he leaves your company. *James blows past his sales quota.
Maloney	"Maloney, increase the menu prices."	*Maloney increases the menu prices by 10 percent.	"Maloney, we need to make ten percent more per square foot in every brick-and-mortar location."	*Maloney decides to create more seasonal offerings instead of increasing prices. As a result, he attracts new customers, retains old customers, and revenues increase even more than 10 percent.

Once you set the outcome instead of telling your employees "how," they start talking about results, not tasks. They begin offering their energy, not just their skills. They start asking themselves, *Is there a better way?* instead of asking you, "How do we do this?"

When you lead through the outcomes you want to see in your company, you are not in charge of the solution. They are. In the end, just like with Adam, they should be bringing you possible solutions (or, better yet, solving problems without your involvement). The Buy-back Principle—Don't hire to grow your business. Hire to buy back your time—then begins to take root as you reclaim time and energy you once spent on other outcomes.

~~Check~~ Measure

If you've ever coached children on a sports team, you understand exactly how numbers motivate and provide clarity. You could show kids on your volleyball team how to bump, set, and spike all day long, but until you explain how they score, they won't care. As soon as you describe the points system, and how to win, their internal lightbulbs come on as that numerical value ignites performance.

The same thing is true with your employees. Key metrics provide clarity, and they help your employees get crystal clear on their objectives.

In *Moneyball*, Jonah Hill's character, Peter Brand, is a statistical genius. He uses complex mathematics to help the Oakland A's pick the perfect team, but in the end "it's about getting things down to one number."[2]

My good friend Evan Hambrook is the fixed operations manager at Volkswagen Moncton. He told me that they have one specific metric they use to measure a dealership's success—their absorption rate. Profit margins on car sales can be relatively small, so dealerships often make up a lot of their income from their parts and service departments. Absorption rate explains the ratio of how much income parts and service is bringing in that covers the dealership's overall expenses. That's their "one number."

Another friend, Janelle, is a hotel manager. When I asked her how she measures success in her field, she immediately piped in, "With the average daily rate (ADR)!"

There are a variety of room rates a hotel offers at any given time—preferred rates given to online travel sites like Travelocity and Expedia, discounted room rates for AAA members, free upgrades for elite members, et cetera. But in the end, Janelle only needs to know one thing: average daily rate.*

---

* Some lodging establishments may use the average room rate, or ARR, but the concept is the same.

Both Evan and Janelle know their one number and how that number helps drive success. Janelle doesn't have to go through tons of datasets. She just looks at their average daily rate. Evan can compare a dealership's current absorption rate with last year's rate and easily determine if they're trending in the right direction.

Every person in your company needs a similar measurement. These can vary between individuals or teams. While the *overall* goal for your entire company is probably to increase profits, each team or member needs one number they can directly impact. For each sales representative on your team, you could use their quarterly revenue, but for your sales manager, you'd maybe use sales velocity rate.*

Once you give everyone in your company a measurement, here's the good news: their motivation instantly increases. They know how to win, and they get focused quick. Often, they won't need you to help them determine their own success. Often, they can look at their scoreboard and self-correct because they know what they're aiming at.

Give everyone a number, and watch the score go up.

Next Coach

A good coach makes all the difference.

In 1948, UCLA called John Wooden and offered him the head coaching position of the Bruins basketball team. After almost two decades, the team had never won a national title. The school was Wooden's second choice, but he said yes anyway.

He coached the team to their first national title. Then he coached them to another, then another, blowing away not just the school's records, but all NCAA records. To date, no other team in NCAA history has ever won more than two consecutive titles. Wooden won seven in a row.

---

* Sales velocity rate is a number determined by a formula that includes how a prospect turns into revenue.

But he still wasn't done.

By the time he retired, in 1975, his nickname was the Wizard of Westwood, and he'd delivered ten national titles, seven of them consecutive, as well as four perfect seasons.

Today, the Bruins still hold the record for:

- Most NCAA national titles
- Most NCAA national titles in a row
- Most undefeated seasons in history

All these Bruins records are from one man: Wooden. Since he left, the Bruins have won only *one* national title. In their case, success didn't come from the players alone—the coach was key.

> **If you want to have a high-performance team, learn how to coach successfully.**

Coaching your teammates isn't an option—it's a requirement. Managers check off tasks, bark orders, and create reports. *Leaders* know how to pull the best out of someone. They can see potential and make it a reality. Without the coaches, many of the greatest names in sports wouldn't have achieved what they did. For every Michael Jordan, there's a Phil Jackson. For every Simone Biles, there's an Aimee Boorman. For every Steph Curry, there's a Steve Kerr.

Likewise, you need to coach your team.

You build the people, and the people build the business.

CO-A-CH Framework

Coaching has become an overused term, a cliché. Everyone tells you to do it, but no one shows you how. With transformational leadership, you aren't micromanaging—you're putting the majority of the work on the individual. You're setting the goalpost and letting them do most of the work to get there.

But when you see something that is holding them back—an Achilles' heel or a large mistake—you do want to step in, help them overcome the obstacle, and keep them moving forward.

In essence, coaching often comes down to a series of small conversations at pivotal moments that help adjust someone's steering. You can use this CO-A-CH framework for every coaching conversation you have (often called one-on-ones).

The CO-A-CH Framework

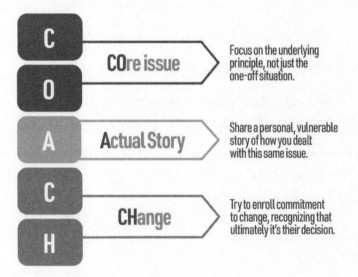

C
O   COre issue   Focus on the underlying principle, not just the one-off situation.

A   Actual Story   Share a personal, vulnerable story of how you dealt with this same issue.

C
H   CHange   Try to enroll commitment to change, recognizing that ultimately it's their decision.

I use this coaching methodology *in every single* one-on-one I have. Notice that I focus on the broader issue—the core principle—instead of the one-off situation. Also, I focus on exactly *one* issue at a time.

Here's a real example:

Recently, Kori punted on a decision that she should have made, costing her team a few days in productivity. I noticed it when it happened, but I didn't say anything immediately. Instead, I jotted down what happened so I could mention it to Kori at our next one-on-one.

While coaching her, I reminded her of the scenario. I explained my general philosophy—that the faster we make decisions, the quicker we can execute on goals, make more money, and save time and energy (**CO**re issue). Then I shared a vulnerable story about when I had been prone to hesitating on important decisions (**A**ctual story). "It took a mentor to pull me aside to yank me out of that mindset," I shared. My mentor had explained to me that my hesitation was costing us productivity. I then left it up to Kori, and asked her what she'd need next time to feel comfortable executing on a decision (**CH**ange).

Notice the path I followed to enrolling Kori's buy-in:

COre issue: hesitation affects productivity

Actual story: true story of when I hesitated

CHange: asked Kori what she needed to act decisively next time

In transactional management, you're micromanaging every decision. In transformational leadership, you're helping your teammates make better decisions in the long run.

*

IF YOU WANT to build a lasting organization, you've got to learn to transform your team instead of just managing tasks. Think about how a coach would help you.

If a coach were to help you run a marathon, here's what they'd do:

Set the **outcome** (complete the 2023 Boston Marathon)

Measure your weekly progress with a **metric** (miles run per week)

Then **coach** you to success ("Don't run so hard in the beginning, or you'll gas yourself out.")

Accomplishing business goals works the same way. As a transformational leader, describe the outcome, offer a metric, and coach to success.

Importantly, this is an exercise in patience—transactional management may be easier to do *today*, but it will eventually lead to frustrated employees who feel micromanaged and may eventually quit, costing time and money. With true transformational leadership, you can create lasting change.

5 Buyback Rules

1. Smart leaders don't tell others *how* to do something. They tell them the end results that need to be achieved. Then they allow the other person to use their individual creativity to figure out the how.
2. Every person in your organization, from the frontline worker to the CEO, has responsibilities, their own individual "monkeys." When given the chance, humans are prone to putting their monkeys onto others, and we're all prone to adopting their monkeys too easily. Don't. Ensure that each person is empowered to handle their own responsibilities.
3. Many leaders manage their organization by telling staff what to do, checking their work, then explaining what to do next. That's transactional management. If you do this, eventually the entire organization will come to you for answers on what to do next, and you'll hit the tell-check-next ceiling.
4. Instead, you can embrace transformational leadership, in which you give an outcome, offer a metric to measure progress, then coach to success. In this way, you're joining the employee along a

journey in which they ultimately grow and learn to make decisions without much involvement from you.

5. Use the CO-A-CH framework to coach your staff to success when needed.

The CO-A-CH Framework

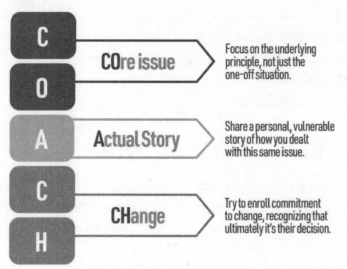

CORe issue — Focus on the underlying principle, not just the one-off situation.

Actual Story — Share a personal, vulnerable story of how you dealt with this same issue.

CHange — Try to enroll commitment to change, recognizing that ultimately it's their decision.

Step into the Arena

This next week, I want you to embrace the CO-A-CH framework. This will help give you a quick win with transformational leadership.

A. Think about that one person in your organization who needs to improve. What's the *one thing* they could do that would up their game? Write that down.

B. Schedule a one-on-one with them.

C. Use CO-A-CH to focus on the **CO**re issue, share an **A**ctual story about when you faced this problem, and then try to get an agreement to **CH**ange.

CHAPTER 12

This "F-Word" Will Save Your Business

HAVE YOU EVER HAD ONE of those really embarrassing moments that became a great story later? Perhaps you came out of the bathroom with toilet paper on your shoe at a conference, or showed up to a formal wedding in shorts and a polo shirt. "Neil" made one of those "I wish I had kept my mouth closed" mistakes.

Jacob had been working for Neil for about three months as an automation expert, connecting certain programs together to ensure they were . . . well, automated. Neil wasn't happy about Jacob's performance. After three months, he was tied up in knots about it. But he never said a word to Jacob.

Neil hopped on a conference call with members of his marketing department, who began giving him updates on various projects. Neil's Zoom settings were set so that he could see only the first five people who joined the meeting. He didn't bother scrolling past those five to see who else was on the call. The team began giving updates.

Neil found out that for one project, marketing was *still* waiting on an item that Neil assumed was Jacob's responsibility. Neil was fed up and started complaining about Jacob. Toward the end of Neil's mini-rant about Jacob, a familiar voice chimed in:

"Hey, it's me, Jacob. I'm on the call."

I know that stung Neil. Because Neil's real name is *Dan Martell*.

*

INSTEAD OF CONFRONTING Jacob directly, I had brushed it off and embarrassed myself (and Jacob) in front of an entire department. I'd let all the emotions of his past performance build up. Instead of giving him some quality feedback, I'd just sat, brewed, and stewed. In two minutes, three months' worth of frustration came out because I hadn't created a space where we could have two-way dialogue.

A Human Ticking Time Bomb

I hadn't discussed my problems with Jacob in a healthy way—but the bigger issue is that I didn't know about any issues Jacob had with me.

- Maybe he had too much work on his plate.
- Maybe he didn't understand his role.
- Maybe he was working on another project I didn't know about.
- Maybe he *thought* he was doing everything correctly, and I just never gave him the chance to change any of it.

I'd failed at creating a relationship where feedback was expected and fluid. I'd chickened out on giving Jacob feedback and never allowed Jacob to offer feedback to me. I'd missed the critical "F" word in business.

No Feedback = No Productivity

Do you want your whole company to get back to producing high-energy results?

Then ensure that feedback is flowing freely. A lack of two-way communication and feedback can become a culture cancer and spread throughout the entire organization, causing major issues.

We talked about Keith Ferrazzi in chapter 6. In his book *Never Eat Alone*, he discusses a time when he suddenly was unable to find time in his boss's calendar for important meetings. Frustrated, he investigated. The problem? Ferrazzi's right-hand staff member was butting heads with his boss's administrative assistant. This future *New York Times* bestselling author could have lost his job over a small issue.

I wish my embarrassing mistake with Jacob were the only time I'd ever chickened out on a conversation, only to explode later. But I'd done the same thing, just a couple years before, with worse consequences.

In 2012, I hired a new full-time employee, Alexis. She'd been contracting with us for a while as a specialist, doing excellent work, so I brought her in-house to lead our marketing department. But one month in, Alexis wasn't performing—nothing seemed different in marketing. Whether she showed up to work or not, we had the same amount of leads and opportunities. I noticed the problem, but I didn't say anything. *Well, she's a new mom. I'll just let it slide.*

Three months went by, and still nothing had improved. I considered talking to her, but I never got around to it.

Eventually, after six months, I had to let Alexis go. At the time, I believed I was making the correct—albeit difficult—decision. Alexis was underperforming for half a year, so I had to let her go find where she was a better fit.

But looking back, I can see I made the same mistake with both Jacob and Alexis: in neither case did we feel comfortable giving each other feedback. If we'd had a better relationship, maybe I could have learned of an easily fixable issue. Perhaps Jacob needed a tool or piece of software we didn't currently have. Maybe Alexis didn't understand her new role and what she was responsible for. Perhaps Jacob was unclear about deadlines. Maybe Alexis was getting too much work put on her from other departments, and she didn't know how to say no. In any case, I don't know because I never asked them.

In both cases, for months, productivity was stalled, and people's careers were put in jeopardy, when perhaps the only thing needed was some feedback—from me to them, or them to me.

Unlocking Team Performance Again

In 2021, in what's been dubbed The Great Resignation, an unprecedented number of US employees left their jobs. In one month alone (July) four million people quit, and *half* of all US employees said they were considering leaving.[1,2] What were they all looking for?

It's easy to guess things like more money, professional and personal development, better pay, and better work environment. But even more than those items, people want meaning and purpose in their work. According to a McKinsey & Company study, 70 percent of employees find their life's purpose *inside* their job.[3] A similar study by PricewaterhouseCoopers (PwC) listed "meaning in day-to-day work" as the top reason frontline employees want to work somewhere. Think about what that means for you.

Your employees are literally hoping to find *their life's purpose* inside their job. They aren't just looking for Ping-Pong tables or better coffee makers. They want to do something that has impact.

Consider if you got everyone lined up, doing what they love, bringing their passion and energy into work because they *did* find that purpose. Again, effective communication matters here.

Let's go back to Alexis. Remember, she had been performing great in her previous role. Maybe she was great as a part-timer but not as a full-timer because she was more suited to the previous work schedule. If I had asked her what the issue was, maybe she would have told me.

While you may not always be able to provide every employee with exactly what they want, oftentimes with some simple feedback you can think creatively to get them resituated.

If you have a smaller company, you probably have *lots* of tasks that need to be performed. If you can find out what each of your employees loves to do, then productivity will accelerate. If you have a larger company, you probably have various formal roles available, and if a talented player isn't enjoying their current work, why not swap them into a different position? I've moved several of my "A" players because they're hardworking, motivated, but there was a better seat for them on the bus.

> In general, most companies have a buffet
> of work available—so why not get everyone
> their favorite dish?

Again, the only way you're going to know if someone on your team needs to redirect their efforts into a different task is if they feel comfortable speaking with you. And that starts with you.

Can You Handle the Truth?

Small problems, such as missed deadlines, misunderstandings, and interpersonal issues, are inevitable in a work environment. Don't avoid them. Use them.

Kim Scott, author of *New York Times* bestseller *Radical Candor*, notes that at Alphabet (formerly Google), dissension is actually *encouraged*. Alphabet knows it's better to hear about a problem in a boardroom than it is to hear about it from the market.

I tend to agree with Alphabet. If a sales representative is frustrated that she's never getting qualified leads from the marketing team, maybe it needs investigation. If an employee is frustrated with his workload, maybe he needs help in tweaking his work style. Allowing these issues to surface—or better, *encouraging* them to surface—will save you loads of time and energy in the long run.

Think of it like traffic on a highway—each small problem is one more car on the freeway. As long as some of them are constantly exiting, you can keep up the high speed. But if too many cars build up, everything comes to a grinding halt.

Matt Mochary, author of *The Great CEO Within*, offers the perfect model for creating an organization where feedback freely flows from one person to another.

I asked Matt to join me on a conference call with my coaching clients. It took me several requests, but finally he agreed. He didn't disappoint. Instead of just offering the steps, he had us perform a feedback session live. After Matt gave me a summary of his framework on our conference call, he put me in the hot seat.

"Dan, let's demonstrate this feedback framework, live, for all your coaching clients, right now, on this call."

I was a little hesitant, but I jumped in. Watch closely what Matt did because it's genius.

"Dan, can you please share with me one thing that you liked about what I said today during this call?"

I offered some fairly benign information, telling him I liked the way he used stories.

"Thanks, Dan! That's really helpful," he said. But he was just getting me warmed up.

"Dan, I bet you know of something I could do to *improve*. Here's what I want you to do: Just *think* about that one thing I could do. You don't have to tell me yet, just think about it."

I thought of something immediately. Then Matt said, "Okay, Dan, can you go ahead and share it with me?"

I felt awkward, but I told him anyway. I explained that I thought it was unfair of him to initially refuse my invitations to hop on a call because of his reasoning that "I don't do big groups." That bothered me. I thought that was a bit selfish. He is an expert at something, so why not share it? To me, that's big, because it's part of my ethos: learn, do, teach.

Matt responded politely and thanked me for the feedback. Then he told me that he "accepted" my feedback. The person receiving feedback—in this case Matt—should always listen to the feedback, but then they have a choice: accept or reject it. Matt could have rejected my feedback because he had a legitimate reason beyond selfishness for refusing to hop on a call with me. Listening is always key, but whether or not the feedback gets implemented is up to the receiver.

Matt also asked me if there was more feedback that I hadn't told him, a key ingredient. Often, particularly when it comes to giving critical feedback to leaders, people are shy. Even when they do warm up to the idea and start to share, they often don't open up all at once. They crack the door, just inching their foot into a room that they're scared to enter. If you invite them all the way in, sometimes there's a lot more they have to say.

Oh—and here's an added bonus—after Matt asked for my feedback, I instinctively felt the urge to ask him if he had any feedback for me.

Typically, after you've made someone feel safe offering you feedback, they naturally feel the urge to ask you the same question, getting you one step closer to creating a culture where feedback flows freely.

Putting CLEAR into Practice

I call what Matt was showing me a clearing conversation, and I've outlined the specific steps below. I know—we just used the CO-A-CH framework last chapter, so CLEAR may feel a little cheesy. But it's a mnemonic device that stands for Create, Lead, Emphasize, Ask, and Reject (or accept).

While Matt and I demonstrated this live, feedback dialogue between a leader and an employee is typically best done in a one-on-one session. This also assumes that the leader is the one initially asking for the feedback from their employee.

C *Create a warm environment.* Invite them to share a piece of positive feedback first. It's tough for them to offer critical feedback. However, they'll probably think it's easy to say something nice. So after they give you positive feedback, you can ask them to think— but don't say out loud—that one bit of cringe-worthy feedback they could offer. All you're doing here is creating a warm environment.

L *Lead them to offering critical feedback.* Now that they're thinking about that negative feedback, ask if they don't mind sharing it. You can tell them that you already know you're not perfect, but hearing some criticism might help you improve. Tell them your goal is to become a better leader.

E *Emphasize.* Take it in. You don't have to accept it, just listen. Make sure to repeat the feedback back to them, in your own words, so they know you really got it. Making them feel heard and understood is 80 percent of the value of this framework. After repeating it back, ask them if you got it right.

A *Ask if there's more.* People often lead with something small. Give them one more chance to share the real deal.

R *Reject or accept the feedback.* Here, you can either accept or reject what they have to say. If you accept it, make a commitment for how you'll change your behavior going forward. If you don't accept it, thank them for the feedback.

If you want to optimize your organization, these CLEAR steps help to remove roadblocks and start the work of building a feedback-driven organization. Start with your direct reports over a few months as you connect and have one-on-ones with them, and eventually suggest they also follow this flow with their direct reports once you've demonstrated the value to them. Don't force it. Suggest it. Invite them to try it out and report back. Using clearing conversations will help remove little problems that could later cause explosions (like my situation with Jacob!).

Saving "A" Players and Hundreds of Thousands of Dollars

Think about how much time and money gets lost when a company has turnover:

- When someone quits, replacements can take months to find and train.
- When an experienced employee leaves, years of company-specific knowledge and expertise leaves with them.
- When staff go to a new company, they're transferring years of company knowledge, industry experience, client relationships, and training to their new role.

Overall, turnover means you're resetting the clock on training, expertise, and relationships.

Conversely, when star players stay, newer employees get up to speed quicker, client and partner relationships grow, and the whole team attracts more and more talent. It's like putting the whole company in the Production Quadrant. Here's how you get your best players to stay: create a real environment where they can gain professional and personal feedback from their peers.

At every other quarterly off-site meeting, our executive team provides each person with direct, honest feedback. We all make a list of every person on the team. We write down one thing they do well and one thing they can improve on. Then we take turns hearing everyone's feedback about themselves.

During one of these, Michael heard *six* people tell him the same thing: that his communication style was confusing. They each explained that, for months, none of them had understood his regular reports. Michael was shocked. He pulled me aside and said, "No one's ever told me that I have trouble communicating." But Michael's also a rock star. You know what he did next? He studied up on better communication, buying some top books on the subject.

The next time Michael offered a team-wide report, he had visual aids, detailed analyses, and clear bullet points. Overnight, Michael became a communication all-star, simply because the team gave him the opportunity to improve.

When a company builds a culture of feedback, everyone wins. Small issues evaporate before becoming larger, projects don't get stalled by communication errors, and individuals can thrive.

But all of that starts with one simple step: when the leader invites the feedback. You have to be willing to go first. Giving feedback is way easier. Asking for honest and critical feedback regardless of the reason takes guts. That is where the magic is.

5 Buyback Rules

1. When team members, including you, keep issues inside, someone is bound to explode. Leaders will often explode on their employees, which can have devastating consequences. Employees, too often, will just quit if they aren't allowed to voice their concerns.
2. In a culture of low feedback, productivity will slow. Small, interpersonal issues will halt forward progress.
3. In a company with a high feedback culture, progress accelerates, as people feel heard, seen, and appreciated.
4. Feedback can be difficult to give and receive. The founder must set the example by first asking others to offer feedback. Then the leader must listen. As others feel comfortable offering their leader feedback, even critical feedback, they'll see that their opinions are heard and validated. As a bonus, they'll often be more receptive to receiving criticism.
5. The CLEAR steps can help defuse the awkwardness of offering clearing conversations. This is best done, at first, in a one-one-one environment where the leader invites feedback:

- Create a warm environment.
- Lead them to offering critical feedback.
- Empathize.
- Ask if there's more.
- Reject or accept the feedback.

Step into the Arena

I guarantee that your employees have some suggestions for their leader. (Think about how much feedback you have for them. Then realize they feel the same way about you!) The only way you can improve is if you hear them out. Here's your homework:

A. Schedule time to meet with two to three of your direct reports in the next month, if you don't have meetings set up with them already.

B. At these meetings, ask them to offer you feedback. It may be awkward at first, but use the CLEAR steps. You'll get the hang of it.

C. Tip: Just listen. If nothing else, try to see their perspective and think about it. You don't have to implement any changes right away. (But if you keep hearing the same thing from every single person, you might want to!)

CHAPTER 13

Dream BIG. Achieve Bigger

If you do not know where you are going, you will end up exactly there (where?). If you fail to plan, you plan to fail. If you have no specific goals, you will get no specific results.

—DAVID CAMERON GIKANDI AND BOB DOYLE[1]

IN 2003, LANE MERRIFIELD AND his coworker Lance Priebe went to their boss, Dave Krysko, and pitched him their idea. Dave was the founder of a small marketing agency. They worked with high-end clients in the United States and Europe, such as John Deere.

Priebe and Lane had other ideas. Priebe had been up late at night, after work hours, for years, creating mini-games online. As the Internet kept growing and attracting younger and younger audiences, he and Lane had this crazy notion: How could they create a safe space for kids to meet online, chat, have fun, and find community, all in a warm, welcoming environment?

Remember, this was 2003. Much of what they wanted to do hadn't been done before. They'd need to court more than half a dozen banks just to find one willing to let them take payments. Lane also didn't want to make money by the conventional method of online businesses—advertising. Instead, he wanted to try something almost unheard of: a subscription-based model. Lane was adamant about this part—he wanted to create a virtual community with children's safety at the forefront, and allowing a litany of huge corporations to advertise their products and services to young children didn't fit that goal.

Dave, Lane's boss, listened to his employees' two-hour pitch about the new online experience they were going to create. He understood the video game portion and the chat rooms. But when they started mentioning "flash," "servers," and something about penguins, they lost him. After 120 minutes, Lane and Priebe paused and prepared to hand over their resignations. Then Dave said something surprising:

"I have no idea what you guys are talking about. But I've never seen either of you this passionate before. So let's figure out how to do this *here*."

Dave wasn't going to let his employees leave. They were going to take their penguin-based video gaming idea for kids and do it with Dave's—and his whole company's—help.

Dave was better than his word—he basically donated his own business as the seed capital. He told Priebe to dive in full-time, and said that Lane could use any extra revenue he generated in his position at Dave's agency to fund the development. They got to work.

Lane took out a line of credit on his house. Priebe worked all-nighters. They called in a few favors from some colleagues, and pretty soon they had a beta up and running. They figured they could get fully operational by 2010.

They wanted about four thousand accounts for their beta.

Instead, twenty thousand people signed up in five weeks.

So they went live much earlier than they expected, in October 2005.

In less than six months, they had over a million sign-ups, and their bootstrapped company was stretching their computer infrastructure to its limitations. At one point, they paid IBM consultants to come in and look at their own machines to determine how they could keep their servers from crashing. After three days, IBM returned their money.

"We don't know how our machines are performing as well as they are. You're using them in ways we didn't know were possible," they told them.

By 2007, almost 30 million kids all over the world were using Club Penguin, and Lane knew they needed help to keep up with the infrastructure. If they wanted to continue keeping all kids safe, they needed to establish offices across the globe, in different countries with different languages and different technical needs. They started looking for adoption by a larger firm. And then, twenty-two months after Club Penguin went live, Disney purchased the online gaming platform for $350 million.*

To Lane, Club Penguin was pure passion. Disney wasn't even the highest bidder. (Although, to be fair, $350 million has a lot of zeros in it.) Lane sold to Disney because he knew they had the right capabilities to keep Club Penguin a safe and fun online environment for kids.

Like Oprah, my friend Lane found what lights him up, and the world rewarded him.

Turning Impossible to Inevitable

Here's why I like Lane: he dreams big. When Lane talks about Club Penguin's meteoric rise, he doesn't sound like he's talking about a company. He has the excitement of a kid launching a homemade rocket in their backyard.

Everyone doubted him. Reporters mocked him. IBM couldn't help him. But Lane was going to find the way to his destination.

In this chapter, we're going to do something a little different. We've been talking a lot about buying back your time. We've talked about removing the small, tedious tasks in your Delegation Quadrant.

---

* Plus an additional $300 million in payouts if certain goals were met.

We've also discussed how to make sure you don't get sucked into the Replacement Quadrant forever. Now let's talk a little about why it all matters—your Production Quadrant. That's the goal.

While I was writing this book, I hopped on a coaching call with my client Carl. Here's what he told me:

> *Dan, I took your Buyback Principle advice! I hired an as-sistant, then scaled up the Replacement Ladder, and bought back almost all my time! My thirty-minute call with you is the only thing I have to do all day.*

Misunderstandings like that are exactly why I wrote a full-length book. Carl's business was running so smoothly and efficiently, he had less than half an hour of work in an entire weekday. Instead of investing that time into something that would create even more growth for his business, Carl was retiring from life.

I wasn't surprised he'd found time—the Buyback Principle works. But I was upset. "I love you Carl," I told him, "but you need to hear this: I did not help you buy back your time so you can sit on your ass and do nothing to build your empire. You're an artist, and my goal was always to help you unlock another level of growth."

As you find more time, you'll need to learn how to redeposit some of it into the Investment Quadrant. Likely, that's what Carl *thought* he was doing. But he wasn't—and he probably wouldn't have lasted long just idling around, and neither will you. Entrepreneurs can't just retire from life.

> If you're an entrepreneur, you wouldn't last long sitting on a beach. You'd sit your butt in the sand for a whole few days before getting antsy. After staring at that umbrella for too long, you'd probably invent a better one, start a new company, and hire the pool boy as your first employee.

That's the DNA of an entrepreneur.

On one hand, Carl was doing great: he had successfully *audited* and *transferred* his time. But apparently he forgot the last word: *fill*.

Once you start buying back massive time—and if you follow these tactics, you will—how do you fill that time meaningfully?

As you start to buy back your time, you need to deposit it into the Production Quadrant.

And for that you need something big, bold, and meaningful.

I want you to have a huge dream—one like Lane's. In this chapter, I'm going to help you get there.

Importantly, your dream needs to be insanely huge, but it also must be incredibly clear. In the end, you'll need what I call a 10X Vision—something so big, so crazy, so huge, that it inspires you like crazy. Think landing on Mars, winning an Olympic gold medal, selling your company for $1 billion, turning all trash into compost, et cetera.

To ensure that your 10X Vision is both as large as possible and also as clear as possible, you need to break it up into two phases, and we'll go over both in this chapter:

1. **Phase 1: Dream without limits.** Here, you just let yourself go— you don't worry about the *how*, you just focus on the *what*.
2. **Phase 2: Create clear vision.** After you let yourself dream, it's time to add in some clarity.

I separate these phases so that you can dream big, get clear . . . and *then* get practical. When entrepreneurs mix these phases together like a mishmash recipe, they make mistakes.

Let's get started.

Phase 1: Limitless Dreaming

To be clear, when I say *big*, I mean it: Club Penguin was a dream so big that it was just shy of impossible. For entrepreneurs, this is nonnegotiable.

You're going to face problems—I guarantee it. I can't promise that you'll dive into your next venture and succeed, but I can promise you that if your dream is *not* big enough, you won't have a reason to try very hard. Entrepreneurism simply isn't worth the effort unless you're going for the gold.

For one, anything short of a near-impossible dream is simply unmotivating.

In the early 2000s, Dr. Casad, a professor at the University of Colorado at Colorado Springs, opened his freshman psychology class with a startling introduction:

"Hello freshmen and welcome to Psychology 101. I've got some news for you. This class will be *difficult*!"

The students began to grumble.

Dr. Casad went on to describe exactly *why* he made the class challenging.[2] Studies have shown that when something's too easy, people don't apply themselves. They may slack off, procrastinate, or even get bored. Counterintuitively, when a class is challenging, students are motivated to really go for it.

Entrepreneurs are dreamers. If they don't have a dream big enough to work toward, they'll get bored.

Entrepreneurs are also Navy SEAL–level problem solvers. You enjoy solving huge problems so much that if there isn't a problem to solve, you'll make one up. You know what I'm talking about—the chaos addiction that we discussed in chapter 3.

The solution? Set a target worth aiming for.

What do you *really* want? Putting aside what's easy, or even what's possible, what would you dream of if there weren't any limitations?

Lane wanted to create a virtual community for children—one

with a safe chat room, no ads, and pure fun. To many, that was about as possible as space travel. Yet he did it.

Maybe that doesn't interest you, excite you, or motivate you. What does? Spending free time with your family? Buying a yacht? Creating a Fortune 100? Writing ten *New York Times* bestsellers?

As Tim Ferriss would say, "What can you do that would be remembered 200 to 300 years from now?"[3]

In my SaaS Academy intensives, I push my clients to dream insanely huge. Oftentimes, the huge pile of daily responsibilities can cause us to forget why we do what we do at all. And that's a critical mistake for entrepreneurs.

Entrepreneurs are uniquely gifted in their problem-solving abilities. The world's depending on you to use those talents. So in my intensives, in a room full of other passionate (and wild) problem solvers, I give my clients the chance to really dream again. I tell them not to even consider what's possible, and instead, just to let themselves get crazy.

Here are a few of the crazy dreams I've heard:

- Eliminate all trash
- End childhood hunger
- Enable individual human flight

What does "enable individual human flight" mean? I'm not quite sure— but it sounds awesome.

If this all sounds too fluffy, let me give you a few good reasons why dreaming big is not just fun, but essential to your entrepreneurial journey.

Big Dreams Drive Innovation

When you stop dreaming, you lose motivation, but more importantly, your creativity can dwindle. When you reignite your dreams—big ones, like becoming a Fortune 100 company, inventing a new piece of software, or quadrupling your revenue—your creative mind gets to work, quickly. You stop thinking about making an extra $1,000, and you start thinking about landing a thousand more clients. Instead of worrying about how to make a few follow-up calls, you tell your team to go for the big whales. Rather than hoping you can dish out a blog post, you think about writing a few novels.

Think of racing a car around a track: if your goal is to shave off one second of time, you'll practice taking tighter turns and shifting a little better. But the moment you think, *I must **double** my speed*, your brain kicks into high gear. Now it's exciting. You'll need to reengineer your engine, develop new tires, and deal with aerodynamics.

As the saying goes: "Necessity is the mother of invention." The way I see it:

> **The bigger the necessity, the bigger the invention.**

Big Dreams Put a Fire in People's Bellies

If you've ever met someone who's insanely excited about what they're doing, it gets you excited. My friend Josh Elman is that guy.

He's a product genius and software investor who constantly tackles the biggest problems in his industry. I met him in 2010 while he was working with Twitter to upgrade their onboarding experience. Josh couldn't stop talking about what he was doing. I couldn't stop listening.

I hardly used Twitter at the time, but Josh's energy excited me so much, I wrote an entire blog post about it.

Steve Jobs famously poached John Scully, then the CEO of the respected PepsiCo. Jobs wanted Scully to leave his corporate position in his nice office and come join his motley crew of garage heroes. After several unsuccessful attempts to court Scully, Jobs finally said these words: "Do you want to sell sugar water for the rest of your life, or do you want to come with me and change the world?"[4]

Scully quit Pepsi and joined Apple because of Jobs's contagious excitement.

Likewise, you can't hang out with my friends Lane or Josh for very long without feeling inspired to do something. *Passionate people ignite passion in others.*

When you're energized by passion, the way you talk about your goals and the future has a different energy, and there's nothing more contagious than energetic people:

- Customers buy more
- Employees work harder
- Vendors go above and beyond

Go find your passion, then pass it on.

Big Dreams Crush Distractions

Here's what I love about people with insanely huge goals: they know what to put in their calendar, how to spend their days, and what to fill their life up with. They aren't getting haunted by despair or stuck in the mediocre. Every decision in their life relates back to making their insane dream a reality. While other people are wondering what TV show they're going to binge on Tuesday night, dreamers don't even have time for that.

When you find what's lighting you up like crazy, what makes you so excited you can't wait to get up in the morning, trust me, you won't want to watch Netflix, struggle with giving up video games, or even think about wasting time. Instead, you'll probably need to remind yourself to take a break (which is important—see 7 Pillars of Life in the appendix!).

Big Dreams Make Decisions Simple

Once you get real about your big dream, decisions like these will no longer cause anxiety or eat up time:

- Should I hire candidate A or candidate B?
- Which clients should we pursue?
- How should I reorganize my company?
- What opportunities should we consider?
- Where should we put our research dollars?
- Which new marketing should we invest in?
- Should this employee be fired or given another chance?

Business author and coach Dan Sullivan says this: "10X is easier than 2X."[5] Here's what he means:

The key that unlocks success is zooming out of our everyday problems and looking at them more holistically. It's the first lesson you learn in defensive baseball. When a pop fly is coming your way, take a step back. *Always.* When you remove yourself from the agonizing, smaller details and look at your overall goals, connected to a worthy, difficult challenge, your motivation increases, and the necessary steps are really easy to see.

When your dreams are huge, you don't get paralyzed by the in-between stuff. Oftentimes, just having a clear North Star gives you the answer. You know you'll need positive people on your journey, so you can't hire Negative Nathan, even if he's top talent. You know you'll need to go for the most innovative opportunities because anything short of disruptive won't cut it.

Set your North Star and start moving forward.

Phase 2: Create a Clear 10X Vision

Once, I was speaking with Denise, the CEO and entrepreneur of a women's nonprofit. She had a nonprofit that sheltered abused women. But like all dreamers, she was facing some bumps in the road.

She started sharing with me a few problems in her organization. Instead of addressing those issues directly, I asked if she had a clear idea of where she wanted her nonprofit to be in the next decade.

"Do you have a clear vision on where you want your organization to be in the future?" I asked Denise.

"Sure! In ten years, we'll expand into more cities and hire more staff to help many more women who need our services."

Good start, I thought, *but not quite there.* This vision wasn't clear at all. Her goal was more like a vague pipe dream. So I changed tactics and asked her a different question. I asked her to describe her organization's *current* situation. Instead of listing generalities, she got really specific, really quickly:

"Currently, we're in four cities. We have thirteen shelters that each hold up to four people. I have twelve people on staff, and ten volunteers who help on the weekends." She kept going with dates, figures, and more specificity.

That's a clear description—and that's the kind of description she needed to have for her future vision. With a crystal clear picture in her mind of what she was after, many of her organization's problems today would map to the right solutions.

I left her with this:

> "When you can describe your future with the same level of detail as your present, you'll have a compelling vision."

From Daydreaming to Vision Building

Athletes win because there is an actionable, clear target—a score-board. People finish marathons because there is a finish line. The problem with many of our dreams is that we wouldn't even know if we achieved them.

We're all prone to losing motivation somewhere between point A and point B. At first, everything is fun to start, and many of us feel excited to finish well, once the end is in sight. But in the *middle* of pursuing our goals, we often lose sight of why we started down a path. People start going to the gym in January but give up by springtime. They say "I do" with every intention of being a great partner, but settle for an unhappy marriage. They fully intend on going back to school, but they never get around to it.

A 10X Vision is simply a wild dream that you've turned into a *clear picture.*

While a *dream* (Phase 1) is the imaginative spark that can moti-vate you temporarily, sort of like a general outline, a final 10X *Vision* is much clearer and more specific. You take that crazy dream, and you add in dates, numbers, and facts. You fill in the people, the places, the events that must occur for that dream to be a reality. Basically, you step into that dream, and you look around, asking yourself, *When this dream comes true, what friends are surrounding me? Where do I live? What does my house look like? What are people saying about me? How old am I? How much money is in the bank?*

Lane created a safe place for kids across the globe to find commu-nity. Madam C. J. Walker became the first self-made female millionaire in American history.* Elon Musk's company became the first private company to send humans into orbit.†

All of those are clear. They have facts attached, details that round

---

* Plus, she did it as a Black woman in the 1910s.

† Elon Musk's company SpaceX was the first private company to send an *orbital* crew. Another private company, SpaceShipOne, sent the first *suborbital* crew in 2004.

out the vision. When you add in the details, and get specific, you can imagine, almost *taste*, what achieving your dream will actually feel like.

I have a detailed picture of my own future. When I say detailed, I mean it: I had my graphics team create a *New York Times*–style front page, complete with several stories about our future company and what we're up to twenty-five years from now. I included awards I've won, revenue numbers, and pictures of my future office (stock photos of happy professionals working together). The specificity makes it real. I can open up that PDF and read future stories of what my team's up to.

Is my level of detail a bit odd? Sure. But as Yogi Berra said, "If you don't know where you are going, you'll end up someplace else."

When you get clear on your vision, everything changes. Current problems become small, creativity starts pumping, and conversations get interesting. But none of that can happen without *clarity*.

Schooling's Clarity

Perhaps one of my favorite stories of someone getting really clear on what they were after is the story of Olympian Joseph Schooling.

At his final Olympic Games in 2016, Michael Phelps did what he always does. Win. By the time he left Rio de Janeiro, he'd added handsomely to his accomplishments, finishing his career with a total of thirty-nine world records and twenty-one Olympic golds—*five* of which he added that year.

But the story of 2016 that interests me isn't that Phelps won five events. The real story is the one event he *lost*, the 100-meter butterfly.[6] The butterfly is indisputably one of Phelps's best events. He'd been the reigning champion for three straight Olympics. Yet his streak was snapped by an athlete new to the Olympic pool, the young Singaporean, Schooling.

In 2008, when Schooling was a ruddy thirteen-year-old living in

Singapore, he'd dropped his homework at home and ran to a local country club to meet his hero, Phelps.[7] They snapped a photo, one that Schooling was able to keep for years. After that picture, he got serious about swimming. He moved to the United States, enlisted a top-notch coach, and began practicing, for almost a decade.

When he jumped into the Olympic pool with Phelps in 2016, he didn't have the titles or the weight of gold on his neck. Instead, he had the motivation of a 10X Vision—he was very clear on what he was after:

Crossing the finish line before his childhood hero.

Within one second of the starting gun, Schooling took the lead. Forty-nine seconds later he touched the wall, and—here's my favorite part—not only did he win, but for a noticeable moment, Schooling *waited* for Phelps to catch up.

Schooling had no Olympic medals, no worldwide fame, and no world records. But he had one thing going for him—a crazy, clear vision of one day defeating the greatest Olympian of all time.

The 4 Elements of the Entrepreneur's Dream

For Olympians, their 10X Vision is clear by nature—cross the finish line first, lift more weight, jump higher, have a higher score.

For entrepreneurs, we need a little help getting clear on our dreams.

There are four specific elements of an entrepreneur's dream that must be detailed in order to turn that dream into a crystal clear 10X Vision:

- Team
- One business
- Empire
- Lifestyle

211 Dream BIG. Achieve Bigger 211

TEAM

To accomplish your dream, who will be in the room with you? Who will you need to join your team to execute on your crazy idea? Will you need a board of directors? If so, how many people? Who's on it?

I like to think of Steve Jobs's ultrasecretive "Top 100."

Jobs had an exclusive meeting with the one hundred most important people (typically Apple employees) who could help him execute on his wildest plans. Purportedly, this was his group of top talent that made the real magic happen, and every year he'd tap them for a three-day meeting that was "never supposed to exist."[8] (I can't imagine the conversations that happened at those meetings!)

If you dream big enough, you'll need your own team. Who's in it?

ONE BUSINESS

When I go to conferences, I ask newer entrepreneurs about what businesses they're in. They often respond with "I own three [or four, or five, or more]." I love the enthusiasm, but the problem is they haven't given themselves time to become world-class in any one area. Steve Jobs had Apple. Arianna Huffington had the *Huffington Post*. Bill Gates had Microsoft. Lane had Club Penguin.

Each of these individuals directed their energy into one business, and from there they were able to grow. Importantly, they gained the skills, network, cash, human talent, and other resources that allowed them to go on and invest in other areas. For instance, Elon Musk has always been an engineer. He didn't try to be an engineer, cure cancer, be a war general, et cetera. By focusing on one area of his life, he was able to gain massive talent and *then* deposit it into an entire empire.

I want you to dream of being an empire-builder who owns multiple entities, but when you're creating your 10X Vision, remember to first focus on one company and becoming world-class at what lights you up so that you can invest in new opportunities.

EMPIRE

After you've imagined (and you're able to clearly describe) that one business, *then* consider your empire. Again, this should stem *from* your core competencies in your Production Quadrant.

What products do you have? Are you in multiple industries? Are you an investor in some companies and a CEO in another? Is there an overarching purpose that connects all these, or are they distinct interests? What philanthropy will you be involved in?

My friend Brian Scudamore started with 1-800-Got-Junk. After growing it to a huge enterprise (it's now a $300 million business), he started O2E Brands to launch his bigger empire. Now Brian runs several franchises, such as WOW 1 DAY PAINTING and Shack Shine, using many of the ideas and techniques he honed at 1-800-Got-Junk.

Considering the overall empire helps you think about the team you'll need today, the connections and network you'll need to build, and the personal development that you'll need to have.

LIFESTYLE

Transport yourself ten years into the future of your dream life. Then walk around a little bit, get it in your blood, and take in the smells, the sights, the sounds.

What are you doing? Are you an avid runner? Are you training for an Ironman, spending time with your grandkids, living in Paris? What will you be doing outside of work? Will you go on multiple vacations, travel the world, or work with inner-city youth? How will you spend your holidays? Who will you be with, what hobbies will you have, and what'll be recharging your batteries?

I'm just trying to get juices flowing here. But when I say "lifestyle," I mean everything that you could possibly think of. Go crazy here—maybe you want four homes in four different parts of the world, one for every season. Whatever your wildest dreams are, expand them, and don't forget the details.

Put It All Together

Once you've considered all four of those elements, you want to put it all together. As I said, I put all mine together to create my 10X Vision in a PDF document in 2007. (You can check it out at BuyBackYourTime .com/Resources/ to get an idea.)

Kyle, the founder of a proposal-creation software company, built his 10X Vision with InDesign and stock photography. Then he set it as the background on his desktop. When he powers up his computer each morning, he literally sees his future staring back at him: smiling photos of his wife and kids, a big boat he hopes to own, and a lake where he'll spend lazy afternoons with them.

"I don't need to think about exactly how I'm going to get there. I just notice little opportunities when they come up," he said.

Just the act of putting this mental framework on paper gives Kyle a jump start on achieving his dreams.

But don't worry—we can get more specific than that. In the next chapter, we'll go over how to plan your Preloaded Year so that you can map your 10X Vision to plans *today*.

5 Buyback Rules

1. You need a huge inspirational picture of what you're working toward. Entrepreneurs are uniquely situated to positively affect and change the world. Big ideas inspire innovation, excite others, help you overcome distractions, and make many business decisions easier.

2. Phase 1: The first step to creating an inspirational 10X Vision is to dream without limitations. Focus on the *what* without the *how*. Don't worry about how you're going to do it, just consider what you would do without any limits.

3. Phase 2: Big dreams eventually need crystal clarity. Once you can describe your future vision with the same specificity and detail with which you can describe your current situation, you'll have a vision that can motivate you today.

4. Specifically, entrepreneurs need a clear vision that has these four elements: a team, one business, their empire, and their lifestyle.

5. If nothing else, dream big!

Step into the Arena

Your goal is to get crystal clear on your future vision. Again, you need to do this in phases.

> **Phase 1: Just dream.** I suggest going on walks alone, talking to your spouse, reading some inspirational books, and speaking with mentors. Just let yourself really go and consider what you would accomplish if you had no limits.

> **Phase 2: Get detailed.** Once you've dreamed big, start making that dream more specific and detailed. Get out a pen, a paintbrush, a drawing utensil on an iPad, and start drawing and writing about your future dreams. Remember to specifically include your team, your one business, your empire, and your lifestyle.

You may remember the tip about making a vision board in chapter 1. That may help you get a jump start!

CHAPTER 14

The Preloaded Year

STEPHEN COVEY, THE FAMOUS AUTHOR of *The 7 Habits of Highly Effective People*, once gave a demonstration that is popularly known as the "big rocks" analogy.

Covey invited a successful businesswoman on stage. He asked about her work as director of an international firm. Then he poured hundreds of small pebbles into a bucket, saying they represented all the tasks she'd need to execute in order to maintain her current career success. Next, he asked her to fit a few larger rocks into the bucket. Each of these had a label attached, such as "vacation," "family," "spirituality," et cetera.

She struggled to fit in a few of the big rocks, but many never made it in.

Then he offered her a fresh, identical, empty bucket. She started by putting all the big rocks in first and *then* pouring in the small pebbles.

Magically, everything fit this time. Same buckets. Same rocks. Same pebbles. Different results.

The two buckets represent two different strategies. When you start by putting all the small pebbles into your life first, you often don't have room for life's most important events. But when you begin with the larger rocks, it's easier to fit in the pebbles around those rocks.

Don't Miss the Big Rocks

In this final chapter, I'm going to help you ensure that the biggest rocks in your life fit in your "bucket," so you don't miss out on life's important moments.

If you don't plan all your biggest rocks first, others around you may pay the price. For entrepreneurs who don't employ the Buyback Principle, this means you'll end up taking on an extra email, working an extra hour, or missing the weekend with your family. You'll be stuck trying to accomplish what's best for your business and your family all at once. When you miss a big rock that should have been in the calendar, you'll stay up late, miss games, dinners, and other important events to execute on to-dos you could have proactively handled. I know because I did that. One year, I randomly popped by my parents' house because I happened to be in the area. My mom said, "Oh, Dan! Good to see you. Were you coming by to take your dad to dinner for his birthday tonight?!"

My face turned red. "Yup!" I said as I gave my dad a hug. But it was too late—he'd seen the look on my face. He knew his son had totally forgotten his birthday.

In chapter 8, we talked about designing your Perfect Week. Using a proactive approach to your week, you're able to head off many of life's biggest distractions and stay focused on what lights you up and makes you money.

You can take that same strategy and blow it up to a yearly level—with a Preloaded *Year*.

A Preloaded Year is exactly what it sounds like—a proactive approach to your year. Similar to the Perfect Week, using a Preloaded Year means you're acting proactively, choosing how you want to spend your time instead of reacting to the demands of others.

From 10X Vision to Big Rocks

As Covey said, the biggest rocks go into your Preloaded Year first, before anything else. Most of these are pretty obvious: family, faith, friends. We're going to make sure *all* of those get in. But don't forget about one other thing that's also huge—your 10X Vision.

We need to break down your 10X Vision into bite-sized, actionable steps so we can make sure it also makes it onto the calendar. So, before we get into how to preload your year, let's take your 10X Vision and work backward to today.

A. Create Checkpoints

You have the final destination in mind—your 10X Vision. Now work backward from there to specific checkpoints from the goal, back to today. To do this, you'll need to have an idea of *when* you're going to accomplish your 10X Vision. If you think it's in ten years from today, then work backward to five years, then three, then one.

At each checkpoint, consider the same four elements: team, one business, empire, and lifestyle.

One of my colleagues, Randall, envisions owning a full-scale media company, with books, interconnected character universes, and animated films.

So he could walk back to five years and see that he'll need to have written dozens of fictionalized novels, have fully developed character universes, and started producing at least one animated film. At the three-year mark, he'll need at least ten books written, five graphic novels, and connections with film financiers. Within one year, perhaps he'll need to have published one book, developed five to ten new characters, and started relationships with media financiers.

Then he can move on to strategizing.

B. List Tactics for the Next Checkpoint

Once you know what you'll need at each checkpoint, brainstorm the tactics that will help you arrive at each one, starting with the first one.

If after giving it solid consideration you truly have no clue how to start, try sharing your 10X Vision with a few business mentors and ask them for ideas on how you could get there. And then, how you could get to the second checkpoint, the third, and so on. Create a long list of ideas. Don't censor yourself—this is a brainstorm, and there are no bad ideas!

If we go back to Randall, let's say three of his tactics for his next checkpoint include:

- Connect with media moguls on LinkedIn.
- Fly to a media conference in Los Angeles.
- Cold-call Disney, Sony, and Universal Studios executives for advice.

Of course, with a good brainstorming session you'll probably want a lot more than three strategies. Go for ten or twenty; it will just help the next part be that much easier.

C. Score Tactics with ICE

Once you've compiled a list of tactics, you'll need to score each of them to narrow down to what you can realistically start on today.

I like to use ICE to give each tactic a score of up to thirty points:

- Impact (1 to 10)
- Confidence (1 to 10)
- Ease (1 to 10)

Impact has to do with money: What type of financial effect will a particular tactic have on revenue today? (Note: "Impact" means "positive impact." So a *low score* would mean that a tactic has no positive financial return today, or possibly even a *negative* financial return. A *high score* would mean that a tactic will likely bring in a lot of revenue quickly.)

Confidence is simply asking, *How sure am I that this tactic is going to work?* If you're absolutely confident it'll work, it's a ten. If it's a Hail Mary, it's a one.

Ease: How easy will it be for you to implement this tactic? If it's insanely simple, give it a ten.

For Randall, his ICE scores may look like this:

- Connect with media moguls on LinkedIn (ICE: 23).
- Fly to a media conference in Los Angeles (ICE: 20).
- Cold-call Disney, Sony, and Universal Studios executives for advice (ICE: 16).

After you've scored each tactic, select a couple (perhaps two to three of the top-scoring ones) and use those as some of your "big rocks" for the year.* Armed with these big rocks, you're now ready to add them into all your other major life events for the year. Let's go make that Preloaded Year.

Your Preloaded Year

A huge thanks to *Million Dollar Coach* author and CEO Taki Moore, as well as my good friend Dale Beaumont (mentioned in chapter 8), who've helped develop the Preloaded Year. Borrowing from their ideas, here's how I make mine every December for the following year:

---

*For more information on scoring with ICE, go to BuyBackYourTime.com.

Place the Few Big Rocks First

First, I preload my year with life's most important things, the big rocks. No missed birthdays, anniversaries, family vacations, or important business events. And of course any ICE tactics. I plug them all in. If nothing else happens, those things will.

In his book *Make Your Bed*, Admiral William H. McRaven suggests that by making your bed as soon as you wake, you'll have accomplished a task already. Plus, even if your day goes to heck, you'll come home to a warm, made bed.

By putting in the big rocks first for the next year (since I make my Preloaded Year in December), I've already accomplished one task for the next year. Plus, then I'll know that even if the year goes poorly (like 2020 did for so many), I'll still come home to a family whose most important dates, holidays, and celebrations I didn't miss.

What are the big rocks of your life?

When it comes to your personal life, the answers may be obvious: anniversaries, vacations, weddings, birthdays.

When it comes to your business, think of the big rocks as the three to five activities that you *can't* miss in this upcoming year because they drive outsized results. This can vary by company. For some entrepreneurs these big rocks may include a handful of conferences, a couple live streaming events, finishing their book, building out a new software project, undertaking major marketing pushes, creating new partnerships, et cetera. Just ensure that you've captured all the important things that drive growth for your company. That way, you don't unintentionally create conflicts and miss them.

Batch Pebbles into Big Rocks

If there are other do-or-die activities that you simply must complete every year, you can batch these together and turn them into big rocks.

For example:

- Do you need to do soft touches with your VIP clients twice per year? Plan all of your touches in a two-day stretch every six months.
- Should you visit all of your international offices? Schedule to see all of them in one month-long marathon trip around the world.

When you batch items together, they become big rocks that can be easily put into your Preloaded Year. Now they'll get done, and they're no longer weighing on your mind or stealing energy away from your top work.

Add in Maintenance

Dale talks about how athletes preemptively prevent dehydration-induced breakdown—they know that when they start to feel dehydrated, they've already lost 20 percent or more of their performance capacity. So instead of waiting until they feel thirsty, they proactively drink water, rest, and eat to stay at an elite level.

Consider when your energy usually dips, and proactively add in "maintenance" so that you stay in elite-level shape throughout the year. For instance, if you know that every couple months you need a quarterly weekend getaway, add it into your Preloaded Year. Or if you need a break after a long conference, add a three-day weekend after every event. I always plan two days off after my biggest events to recharge.

Insert Pebbles

Once your calendar has all the most important events, you can then fill it in with the next most important events, ones that hold significance but aren't absolutely critical. Often, pebbles include regularly occurring events.

In your personal life, pebbles may include things like weekly date nights, church on Sundays, Thursday-night bowling league, et cetera.

For your business, pebbles may mean items like shipping new software or making a few key hires in your company, recurring one-on-ones, and quarterly board meetings.

By now, you should have a good bit of your Preloaded Year already filled. With all the big rocks in, you'll take up a few weeks here and there. Once you batch pebbles into big rocks, you'll see another significant portion of your calendar fill. By the time you're putting in the individual pebbles, 90 percent of your calendar is likely full.

Don't Forget to Stress Test

You need to stress test your own calendar.

Consider the energy, money, and time that each event will give (or take away from) you. When I look at my Preloaded Year, I watch out for colliding events—those that are too close together. For instance, I never put a family vacation before an important business conference. I know the energy that the business conference demands will distract me while on family vacation. So I schedule family vacations after conferences, when my energy resets and I can focus fully on my family.

Finally, take a look at your calendar and ask yourself the ultimate question:

If I accomplish what's in my Preloaded Year, will I think, "Damn! That was an amazing year!"?

If the answer is "yes," you have a good Preloaded Year.

If the answer is "no," rework the plan.

First, dissect the issue.

Does the current Preloaded Year make you feel overwhelmed? Look where you can afford to add in more breaks—long weekends, staycations, or romantic getaways with your significant other may help.

Does the current plan seem impossible to tackle?
Consider what resources you'd need to accomplish it.
Maybe you need a gym membership, a piece of software,
an additional vehicle. There are plenty of tools you may
need to make this plan work. Can you obtain those
tools? If you can, add dates to obtain those resources. If
you can't, you may need to adjust your plan.

Does the plan jazz you up? If it doesn't excite you and
make you want to jump out of bed, you'll need to rework it, adding in at least one big bold bet that really
gets your motor revved up.

Work the Plan

Once you set your calendar, don't renege on the promises you made to
yourself. You already decided what was most important. Now do it.
Jockeys put blinders on horses to enable their highest performance.
Blinders keep horses on track and optimize a horse's energy for what's
most important—winning the race.

Of course, you're not a horse, and unforeseen opportunities will
arise in your personal or business life, and you may need to adjust to
accommodate for those.

Whenever an impromptu opportunity comes up in my life, my
wife and I use a simple test to determine if it's worth deviating from
our plan. We ask each other: "Is this a 'Hell-yeah!' opportunity?" If it
is, we make the change. If not, we stay on track. Overall, we only
change course about 5 to 10 percent of the time.

Remember when I got the email from my friend about going to
Switzerland with Richard Branson (chapter 3)? That was a definite
"Hell-yeah!" opportunity, and I took it!

There's Always Room for Sand (and Even Some Liquid)

The big rocks analogy has undergone many evolutions. In another popular video, a professor fills a bowl with golf balls, then small pebbles, just like Covey did. But in this iteration, the professor then continues to add sand, and then liquid.[3]

This iteration shows another valuable lesson: there's almost always more time for the little things.

Many of my friends with the most creative personalities worry that if they use the Preloaded Year, they'll miss out on all the spontaneity life has to offer. But I have a secret for you: when you plan, you have far more time for spontaneity and way more creative energy.

Let me show you what I mean.

Disruption strategist Shawn Kanungo got on the phone recently with my team. During the call, he offhandedly made a simple statement, saying, "Dan's prolific. He puts out *so* much content."[4]

I do try to post a ton of content. While much of it is planned, I also post Instagram posts when I have a spare moment. I ride mountain bikes with my best friends through Canada and find time for other, small, unplanned interjections.

I'm able to do all of those impromptu events because I have extra time. I can say "yes" to spontaneity, guilt free, because I know that my big rocks, and even my pebbles, have been planned out and they're going to happen. When I have a Friday open up, I know I can go mountain biking without taking time away from my wife's birthday, my kids' soccer games, or my business conference.

And that's the real beauty of the Preloaded Year. You'll find more time to enjoy life's best moments, with a clear conscience, knowing that all of the most important events are preprogrammed.

*

IN 2007, I CREATED a 10X Vision for my life.

I knew I wanted to be an ideator who invested in multiple businesses with the top employees from across the world. Particularly, I wanted to spend my day bouncing from business to business, checking in with the various leaders in my companies, reviewing meaningful strategic decisions, and solving giant marketplace problems.

For that type of empire, I knew I'd need a digital team whose members could meet online from all across the world. I'd want meeting after meeting scheduled with my leaders and boards. To accommodate those, I envisioned some sort of digital meeting room where one company joined me for half an hour, while the next group queued up.

Back in 2007, digital waiting rooms didn't exist. I didn't care. I just drew a picture of what I thought it would look like on my vision board. Even though I didn't have it all figured out, drawing it made it tangible.

Years later, developers created digital conference calls and Zoom made virtual waiting rooms, just as I'd imagined.

I didn't start by asking myself, *Is this possible?* Instead, I just went for it. But within ten years of writing down my "crazy" idea, I was already living it. Dreaming, envisioning, and, importantly, *planning* made my craziest ideas happen.

I want the same for you.

Everything you've read about thus far has led to this, planning your next big move. Dream big, get clear, and plan your year.

5 Buyback Rules

1. By preloading your calendar with what's most important (big rocks) first, you'll fit in not only those big rocks, but also what's moderately important, and even the fun little parts of life.

2. Counterintuitively, the more planned and scheduled you are, the more spontaneity you can enjoy.

3. Think once. Once you've made your year, don't keep making exceptions.

4. You can use the Preloaded Year to help execute on your 10X Vision. Break down your 10X Vision into five-, three-, and one-year goals.

5. If an ad hoc opportunity does arise, and you're considering changing your plans, ask yourself this question: *Is this a "Hell-yeah!" opportunity?* If it is, it may be worth changing your plans. If it's not, stay on course.

Step into the Arena

Thanks to Dale Beaumont and others, I've created a Preloaded Year template that you can download online at BuyBackYourTime.com /Resources. Use this to create a Preloaded Year that helps you think once and execute.

Now, go play your bigger game.

CONCLUSION

The Buyback Life

My goal is to build a life I don't need a vacation from.
—ROB HILL

MY BUYBACK JOURNEY STARTED IN the oddest way—with laundry.

In my twenties, I was living in Parsippany, New Jersey, pumping out long days and nights running my company Spheric.

I wasn't a genius. I didn't have a baked concept like "Don't hire to grow your business. Hire to buy back your time," but I had determined that I needed more time to spend on my business. I looked around at what was taking up precious minutes on the clock, and you know what I came up with? Cleaning and laundry.

I also didn't really love doing either.

While it felt a little odd, I first started buying back my time by having someone clean my townhome and paying the wash-and-fold to do my laundry.

I ended up with a couple extra hours back in my day. And that's when it dawned on me—too many of us are looking at companies in terms of roles, organizational charts, and whose job is whose.

Instead, we need to be looking at the one asset none of us can create more of: time.

As soon as I started thinking in terms of trading my money for more time, I started seeing the opportunity to make those trades everywhere. I could spend ten hours coding, or I could pay someone to code and spend ten hours building my business. I could build my website or pay a website developer (who's better than I am) to do it, then take that extra time and spend it with my kids. But it all started with cleaning, washing, and folding.

Looking back, I also understand my decisions directly and positively affected others: a house cleaner had a new customer, and a wash-and-fold had a new client. By extension, they could redeploy *their* money to buy back *their* time with the increased income.

That's the beauty of the Buyback Principle in action. It has an exponential ripple effect across the pond.

Once you start grasping the power of the Buyback Principle, you'll see opportunity everywhere—in yard work, in people management, in administration, in simple tasks, in complex projects.

Remember how I use the amazing lady Lisa to sort my mail?

Is it a little odd to pay someone to check your mail? Maybe, but that's another lesson the Buyback Principle has taught me—you've got to get vulnerable with people. I don't know much about dating advice, but I've heard that love experts talk a lot about "opening up" to others. That's actually pretty good advice for business, too.

From hiring an administrative assistant, to the Replacement Ladder, if you want to take advantage of all the Buyback Principle has to offer, you'll need to let others into your life.

For instance, I've taken this buyback thing to another level, and now I have what I call a house manager. Like the name sounds, she's the administrator of my home—she manages everything under my roof. She washes cars, fills up the gas tank, picks the kids up from school . . . and a list of other tasks.

Her position holds the same purpose as my administrative assistant or any rung on the Replacement Ladder. My house manager is there to buy back my time.

Nowadays, I try to do only one of two things: spend time with people I love or create within businesses. That's it.

Letting someone support you in business is one thing. But in your personal life? Most people think, *Forget it. . . .*

Having someone in my home feels invasive.

Others will think I'm a snob if I pay someone to clean.

I can manage all this on my own.

After all, it's my personal responsibility.

I've heard all these excuses.

My friends Mandy and Steve have a mini-empire with plenty of money. But last time I visited, Mandy was outside in the hot sun doing yard work. Maybe she wanted to exercise or enjoy the outdoors. But my guess? She just thought it was her job.

*I **can** do this, and I have the time. Why shouldn't I?*

I get that. But what we don't realize is that when we don't pay someone else to do something we could afford to pay them to do, we're robbing them of a paycheck. Why be so selfish?

Don't get me wrong, I understand how chores build personal responsibility. That's why my house manager, Betty, isn't allowed to clean up after my two sons. She doesn't work for them. She works for me. My children need to learn about personal responsibility. I've learned that lesson by now, and my guess is that you have, too.

Plus, let me tell you—having a house manager is really, really cool.

Every day at 4 p.m. Betty hands me a protein shake in my home office. I look up with a smile and tell her thank you, because by mid-afternoon I'm getting hangry with all my meetings and my hectic schedule.

Oftentimes I'm on a conference call hustling a multimillion-dollar deal, and I see her sneak in. So I stick my hand out without even looking, and Betty passes the shake straight into my hand because she knows my routine.

It's protocol: "Give Dan a protein shake at 4 p.m."

That's the sort of routine you can create in your life with a house manager. Knowing that I won't need to stop and feed my belly in the last hour of my workday saves me headspace and time.

Betty follows other simple rules as well (I'm about to give you a glimpse into the real Dan!). For instance, I like to use floss picks. You know, those plastic ones with floss on one end and a pointy toothpick on the other. Also, I'm a sucker for my favorite brand of gum. So Betty ensures that, in every room and every car, there's a baggie with a new floss pick in it and a pack of my favorite gum. Also, at the edge of my bed every night, I find a fresh bottle of water waiting for me. Lastly, I haven't filled up my own car with gas, or even cleaned it, in years.

Betty also makes our lives amazing when my family travels. She'll fly ahead of us to get everything set up so we don't skip a beat, since she has the Playbooks for how things should be organized.

Like Steve Jobs with his famous turtlenecks, I can decide once about protocols and never think about them again.

I think of my home the same way I think of my business. Spending time filling up my car with gas is time I could be spending with my kids. Cleaning my home is time I could have spent on my business. Paying bills is time I could have spent with my wife. With a house manager, I'm able to opt for the best option.

Maybe you're not at this point in your journey, and this sounds far-fetched. You don't need to start with a house manager, but let me tell you, ending up there will save you a helluva lot of time.

Just look around at the opportunities to start buying back your time today—consider cleaning, taking care of your car, food preparation, yard work, et cetera. These are time-consuming tasks that you could likely transfer fairly inexpensively.

Buying Back for Life

The Buyback Principle isn't an activity you do once, then quit. It's a philosophy—one that requires you to constantly <u>audit</u> how you're spending your time; consider how to <u>transfer</u> time-consuming, low-value tasks; then, importantly, <u>fill</u> your new time with what lights you up and makes you money.

When you use the Buyback Principle correctly, you aren't ultimately just searching for more money, you're upgrading constantly to purpose. You're transferring tasks you don't enjoy to someone else who might so you can invest back in your life.

In 2013, Bryan Borzykowski released an article on the BBC titled "Can Retirement Kill You?"[1] The studies he cited provided startling answers to that question. The moment you quit your job and start living the traditional retired life, you are:

- 40 percent more likely to experience depression
- 60 percent more likely to start taking a prescription drug
- 60 percent more likely to be diagnosed with at least one physical ailment

The moment you stop living, you start dying. My plan is to do the opposite—to live so much, death can't keep up with me. If I retired, I wouldn't start doing what I love. I'd have to quit doing what I love.

On our last couples retreat, my wife asked me a simple question: "What do you think retirement looks like for you?"

"Babe," I said, "you're looking at it."

I'm not a genius, but I've started copying Oprah, Buffett, and Branson. I've learned to apply the Buyback Principle, and I'm still learning new ways to let it challenge me to upgrade my thinking, my time, and my business. Because the Buyback Principle allows me to live the life I want today, I have no plans to retire. Ever. I plan on continually buying back my time, applying the Buyback Principle, and enjoying my life.

I have no desire to sell my company and retire so I can hang out in Italy for three months doing nothing. Today, I can go to Italy for three months and invite my favorite people (who all work with and for me) to collaborate in ways that employ all of our own individual "art classes." My business allows me—in fact, encourages me—to use my own skills to solve real problems with people I love.

For instance, to finish this book, I rented a cabin up in the Canadian Rockies with one of my copywriters, Chris. A few weeks ago, my videographer, Sam, dropped in and, after a video project, crashed at my place for a few days. This week, I'll spend Thursday night dating the world's most beautiful woman (my wife), just like I do every Thursday night. I'll go mountain biking with my friends, just like I do every week. I'll spend ample time with my two boys, just like I do every week. I also like going hot-tubbing, so I'll spend an hour a day in the hot tub relaxing, reading books, and feeding my mind with new and cool ideas.

Why retire from any of that?

I invite you to stop waiting for retirement to build the life you want.

Your Empire

When you apply the Buyback Principle to your life, you will find capacity. I guarantee it. From the moment you find your Buyback Rate in chapter 2—you'll begin to think creatively about finding yourself more time.

The more you apply what you've learned, the more time you'll have.

Apply the Buyback Principle, and you won't need—or want—to retire. That gives you a bigger *window* to build the empire of your dreams.

Apply the Buyback Principle, and you'll feel energized at work. That will give you more *energy* to build the empire of your dreams.

Apply the Buyback Principle, and you'll find more days in your week. That will give you more *days* to build the empire of your dreams.

Also, remember: dream *really* big, 10X Vision–style.

I plan on living well into my hundreds. From 2022 until I hit the three-digit mark, I've got about sixty years left. In that amount of time, I can continue building a *huge* empire.

Stop planning on permanently clocking out at sixty-five. Instead, start thinking about having sixty-five *more* years to create. As Colonel Sanders, founder of Kentucky Fried Chicken, once said, "Work is the basis of living. I'll never retire. A person will rust out quicker than they'll wear out."

When you're never going to retire, there's a lot of time to execute on your Production Quadrant.

- If you own a mechanic shop, what would it look like if you franchised that business into every major city in your country?
- If you're a lawyer, what would it look like if your phone number was on a billboard on every major highway?
- If you're a home builder, how would it *feel* if you built a multibillion-dollar portfolio of properties?

Expanding your mind like this doesn't just happen in a day or two. I know, because my brother Pierre started off the same way, swinging a good old-fashioned hammer. When he came to me for help to build his own business (discussed earlier; Martell Custom Homes), one of my first assignments shocked him.

Me: "On a digital map of Canada, use PowerPoint to put a logo on every major city you want your company in."

With only a few homes built and about $27 in the bank, he looked at me like I was insane.

But he did it.

Today, his company has offices in four cities, he's built hundreds of homes, won many awards, and he's well on his way to building out his real estate portfolio. By creating something tangible, a map with pins, he was able to give his dream some legs. It went from a hope to a tangible goal. Now it's time to turn *your* vision into reality. I don't want you to read this whole book, then walk away, doing nothing. I want you to start *now*.

Remember your 10X Vision exercise we went through in chapter 13?

We didn't develop it only to leave it gathering digital dust inside your Google Drive.

Let's step right into it.

We are going to prime your brain to grasp opportunities that'll help you create the life you want. We are going to give you permission to imagine yourself as being something greater than you might have imagined in the past. Here's a quick exercise to start your new life, *now*:

> **Step 1:** Imagine yourself sitting in a movie theater. Put in the details—the size of the screen, the stage, the rows in front of you. Now watch as the movie starts. It's a movie of *you*, living your 10X Vision. In it, you wake up fired up to build your empire. You're focused on your Production Quadrant. Your business runs like a well-oiled machine with Playbooks and "A" players. Your assistant manages your inbox and calendar. Your house manager runs the house. You show up as a transformational leader. No one's in control of your life but you.
>
> **Step 2:** Now get out of your movie theater chair. Walk up to the screen and step into that 10X Vision life. Experience it, letting everything in. Hear the people talking, laughing, and cheering. Feel the clothing you're wearing. Smell the aroma in the air, and sense the tastes on your tongue. Re-create everything that aligns with your 10X Vision, including the expression on your face, your body movements, even your elevated heartbeat.

(By now, your nerves should be firing up like fireworks because your vision has a life of its own!)

Step 3: Here's something no one tells you about visualization: your brain will start rejecting what you're seeing and feeling. It will start drifting into negative thoughts or focusing on *how* your vision could (or, more likely, could not) become a reality. Because it seems so far away. Here, I want you to repeat to yourself: "Thank you, not necessary."

How do I plan on doing this? → *"Thank you, not necessary."*

What will my friends think? → *"Thank you, not necessary."*

This will require so much work! → *"Thank you, not necessary."*

When you have finished this process—it should take less than ten minutes—you can open your eyes and go on with your day. If you make this part of your daily routine, you will be amazed at how much improvement you will see in your life.

As Marianne Williamson said in her mega bestseller *A Return to Love*, "Your playing small does not serve the world. There is nothing enlightened about shrinking so that other people won't feel insecure around you."

"Playing small" doesn't serve you, your loved ones, or any of your relationships. It teaches others to play small. By playing small, you become something less than you might otherwise be. By playing small, you deprive the world of your genius. Instead, be who you can be.

Finishing this book is your vote toward playing a bigger game, stepping into a bigger identity, living a bigger life. Because if you don't, who will?

7 Pillars of Life

A CLIENT OF MINE, AUSTIN, once told me that when he started his company, he abandoned many of his responsibilities as a husband and a father. But, he added, he was doing it for his family. "I told her, for the next four years, I'm not going to be here in the morning when the kids wake up, and I won't be home for dinner," he said. "I need you to hold down the fort, so I can get things turned around and successful."

I asked him why he would do that.

"I did it for them."

"No," I said. "They never asked you for that."

He was a little shaken. He'd never thought about what they wanted. So many founders use "I did it for them" as an excuse for killing themselves at work, often at the expense of their families. But ask yourself:

> What if I reach the top of the success ladder and my family no longer wants me around? What if they become so accustomed to my absence that my presence feels like an intrusion? Is that the lifestyle I want in ten or twenty years?

By missing out on his Investment Quadrant, Austin was working hard, but he was losing some of life's most valuable pieces. (Remember, tasks in the Investment Quadrant light you up, but they don't necessarily make you money, at least not immediately.)

You always want a little bit of time invested here. If not, well, life simply won't be worth living. You'll run so hard chasing after your big dreams that you'll miss the small moments in front of you that really matter—like your children's birthdays, your friend's graduation, or your wife's favorite holiday (guilty).

Time in the Investment Quadrant

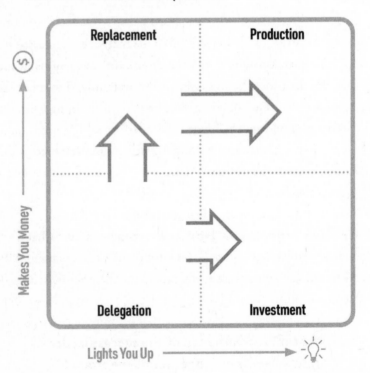

Unlike the Delegation and Replacement quadrants, you always want to be depositing some time into the Investment Quadrant. This allows you to feel healthy and restored.

7 Pillars of Life—A Cheat Sheet

I use the cheat sheet every week to score myself and see how I'm doing. This ensures I don't miss out on what's most important in life as I pursue success.

1. **Health: without it, you've got nothing.** Many people wait until *their body* tells them to quit. (See the story about Stuart in chapter 1.) No matter how much success you have in life, you must have your physical health.

2. **Hobbies: use decompression.** Hobbies, remember those? Running, hockey, perusing the used bookstore for first editions . . . those fun things you used to have time for? When you return from your run, take your skates off, or put down your new favorite book, you feel refreshed. Your face shows it, and so does your attitude. Your hobbies aren't just for you, they're for everyone around you. They're the key to maintaining excellent mental health. Without them, you'll suffer, and those closest to you will, too.

3. **Spirituality: tap into the energy.** This isn't about religion, although it certainly can be. What's most important is that you develop a spiritual connection with the world around you. That could mean meditation, yoga, or going to church.

4. **Friends: don't drop the ball.** Often, entrepreneurs embody the typical type-A personality. You're probably disciplined, hard-working, and focused. But if you don't get your head out of the work and start spending some time with your friends, one day you'll look up and no one will be there for the moments that matter most. Friendships are like muscles: if you don't invest in them, they fade away.

5. **Love: go all in on your relationships.** Half-assed relationships don't work. Period. You need to be all in, all the time. "Love" clearly includes spousal relationships and children, but I think we should

also extend more love through every human connection. How much love is in your home, your work, your life?

6. **Finances: face the money.** I know you're already cringing. Entrepreneurs (like most people) would rather not have another money conversation. You can manage to put your finances out of your mind for the moment. However, they'll always be nagging at you, slowly draining your energy in other areas. Face up to your finances.

7. **Mission: know why you're trying.** People say they want to be successful. But if you ask "What does that look like?" they can't answer. They don't know why their health matters, their work matters, or anything matters. In your business, you need to remember the mission that inspired you to start in the first place.

Before I had these pillars, I used to say that "balance is bullshit." (Crazy, I know.) Then, my philosophy was that you should focus on one major area (such as your business) at a time, and put everything else into maintenance mode. Now I know better. There are certain pillars that can't be ignored because they're the building blocks of your entire life. When one falls, your whole life could come crashing down.

This simple cheat sheet won't solve everything, but it will help ensure that you're keeping some time deposited into the Investment Quadrant along the way.

Here's how I use the 7 Pillars of Life: I score myself on these key pillars *weekly*. Then I pay particular attention to my two lowest scores. Finally, I brainstorm ways I could improve them next week. If I scored low on love, I plan (hopefully, by adding it to my Perfect Week from chapter 8!) how I could do something small for my wife: take her out on a date, give her a night off, or send her for a massage.

Importantly, this isn't a perfect system, but it's a way to help you rapidly deploy new time and energy into Investment without taking a total break from life.

Acknowledgments

THIS BOOK WOULDN'T HAVE BEEN possible without the help of so many people.

First and foremost, I owe so much to my incredible wife, Renée, and our boys, Max and Noah. Thanks for giving me the time, space, and grace as I put in the long hours, writing retreats, and phone calls with the team to focus on this book. To my best friends and business minds, Nick Hansen, Martin Latulippe, Keith Yackey, Brad Pedersen, and to my brother Pierre Martell, who was a sounding board and inspiration for many of these strategies: thank you for the endless conversations on the topics covered in this book. Without your feedback, this book would never have become what it is today.

Then there's my amazing team: Ron Friedman, my "Book CEO," whose call one day inspired this whole crazy journey. Lucinda Halpern, my incredible agent, for dealing with the emotional roller coaster that's required when birthing a book and always pushing for the best outcomes. Paul Fair, my writing partner, who helped bring these words to life. Chris Rigoudis for the five-day editing trip we took to finalize the manuscript and for his incredible support with all his edits and feedback. Rich Gould for helping revise and tweak the designs and models in the book and for being my personal creative director in everything I do. Noah Schwartzberg and the whole team at Penguin Random House for believing in the Buyback Principle and never missing a beat.

Finally there are those who inspired me for so many years to maybe, just maybe, someday write a book: Clay Hebert for his endless enthusiasm and creative thinking. Jayson Gaignard for creating a community of incredible authors who inspired me for years so that one day I would write my own book. Taki Moore for being a world-class coach to coaches and teaching me how to communicate my ideas in a way that's visual and engaging. Tim Sanders, who wrote that first book I ever read, which caused me to fall in love with reading and seeded an idea to write my own book one day. To all my clients and friends who've helped me shape these frameworks and ideas by trusting me to help you in your journey. Your trust in the process meant the world. To all these people: I am deeply grateful.

Notes

Introduction: How Business Saved My Life (Then Almost Ruined It)

1. Stephen R. Covey, *The 7 Habits of Highly Effective People: Powerful Lessons in Personal Change* (New York: Simon & Schuster, 2020).

Chapter 1: How I Buy Back My Life

1. James Clear, *Atomic Habits: An Easy & Proven Way to Build Good Habits & Break Bad Ones* (New York: Avery, 2018).
2. Michael A. Freeman et al., "Are Entrepreneurs 'Touched with Fire'?" (prepublication manuscript, April 17, 2015), https://michaelafreemanmd.com/Research_files/Are %20Entrepreneurs%20Touched%20with%20Fire%20(pre-pub%20n)%204-17-15.pdf.
3. Allan Dib, *The 1-Page Marketing Plan: Get New Customers, Make More Money, and Stand Out from the Crowd* (Miami: Successwise, 2018).

Chapter 2: The DRIP Matrix

1. "Oprah Gail Winfrey: Star Born Out of Adversity," *Hindustan Times*, January 29, 2020, https://www.hindustantimes.com/inspiring-lives/oprah-gail-winfrey-star-born-out-of -adversity/story-a7NN8muJ5lLl22PaOXpFkK.html.
2. Sarah Berger, "Oprah Winfrey: This Is the Moment My 'Job Ended' and My 'Calling Began,'" *Make It*, CNBC, April 1, 2019, https://www.cnbc.com/2019/04/01/how-oprah -winfrey-found-her-calling.html.
3. Kaitlyn McInnis, "Oprah Winfrey Reveals the Universal Way to Know You've Found Your Life's Calling," Goalcast, October 8, 2019, https://www.goalcast.com/oprah-winfrey -reveals-the-universal-way-to-know-youve-found-your-life-calling/.
4. OWN, "Oprah Explains the Difference Between a Career and a Calling | the Oprah Winfrey Show | Own," YouTube, October 13, 2017, https://www.youtube.com /watch?v=opNxqO70smA.
5. OWN, "Oprah Explains the Difference between a Career and a Calling | the Oprah Winfrey Show | Own," YouTube, October 13, 2017, https://www.youtube.com /watch?v=opNxqO70smA.

6. Gay Hendricks, "Building a New Home in Your Zone of Genius," in *The Big Leap: Conquer Your Hidden Fear and Take Life to The Next Level* (New York: HarperCollins, 2010).

7. Jon Jachimowicz et al., "Why Grit Requires Perseverance and Passion to Positively Predict Performance" (prepublication manuscript, February 15, 2018), https://doi.org/10.31234/osf.io/6y5xr.

8. Oprah Winfrey, "A Day in the Life of Oprah," interview by Natasha Silva-Jelly, *Harper's Bazaar*, February 26, 2018, https://www.harpersbazaar.com/culture/features/a15895631/oprah-daily-routine/.

9. Stephen R. Covey, *The 7 Habits of Highly Effective People: Powerful Lessons in Personal Change* (New York: Simon & Schuster, 2020).

10. Simon Sinek, *The Infinite Game* (New York: Portfolio/Penguin, 2019).

Chapter 3: The 5 Time Assassins

1. "London's 1000 Most Influential People 2010: Tycoons & Retailers," *London Evening Standard*, https://web.archive.org/web/20110303202728/http://www.thisislondon.co.uk/standard-home/article-23897620-londons-1000-most-influential-people-2010-tycoons-and-retailers.

2. Melody Wilding, "Why 'Dysfunctional' Families Create Great Entrepreneurs," *Forbes*, September 19, 2016, https://www.forbes.com/sites/melodywilding/2016/09/19/why-dysfunctional-families-create-great-entrepreneurs/?sh=391352b751df.

3. Judy Drennan, Jessica Kennedy, and Patty Renfrow, "Impact of Childhood Experiences on the Development of Entrepreneurial Intentions," *The International Journal of Entrepreneurship and Innovation* 6, no. 4 (2005): 231–38.

4. Steve Blank, "Dysfunctional Family? You'd Make a Great Entrepreneur," *Inc. Africa*, January 9, 2012, https://incafrica.com/library/steve-blank-why-dysfunctional-families-produce-great-entrepreneurs.

5. Wilding, "'Dysfunctional' Families."

6. Steve Blank, "Preparing for Chaos—the Life of a Startup," Steve Blank, April 29, 2009, https://steveblank.com/2009/04/29/startups-are-inherently-chaos/.

7. Wei Yu, Fei Zhu, and Maw-Der Foo, "Childhood Adversity, Resilience and Career Success: The Moderating Role of Entrepreneurship," *Frontiers of Entrepreneurship Research* 39 (2019): 31–36.

8. John Dewey, *How We Think* (New York: Dover, 2003), 78.

Chapter 5: The Replacement Ladder

1. Michael E. Gerber, *The E-Myth Revisited: Why Most Small Businesses Don't Work and What to Do About It* (New York: HarperBusiness, 1995).

2. Joan Acocella, "Untangling Andy Warhol," *The New Yorker*, June 1, 2020, https://www.newyorker.com/magazine/2020/06/08/untangling-andy-warhol.

3. Duncan Ballantyne-Way, "The Long-Lost Art of Andy Warhol and Its Ever-Growing Market," fineartmultiple, 2018, https://fineartmultiple.com/blog/andy-warhol-art-market-growth.

4. Andy Warhol and Pat Hackett, eds., *Popism: The Warhol '60s* (New York and London: Harcourt Brace Jovanovich, 1980), 22.

5. Jennifer Sichel, "'What is Pop Art?' A Revised Transcript of Gene Swenson's 1963 Interview with Andy Warhol," *Oxford Art Journal* 41, no. 1 (March 2018): 85–100, https://doi.org/10.1093/oxartj/kcy001.

6. Acocella, "Untangling Andy Warhol."

7. "The Case for Andy Warhol," The Art Assignment, PBS Digital Studios, YouTube, May 28, 2015, https://www.youtube.com/watch?v=7VH5MRtk9HQ.

8. Blake Gopnik, "Andy Warhol Offered to Sign Cigarettes, Food, Even Money to Make Money," ARTnews.com, April 21, 2020, https://www.artnews.com/art-news/market /andy-warhol-business-art-blake-gopnik-biography-excerpt-1202684403.

9. "Stephen Shore Ditched School for Warhol's Factory," San Francisco Museum of Modern Art, YouTube, May 27, 2019, https://www.youtube.com/watch?v=rPAGGIe4Ln0.

10. "Andy Warhol 1928–1987," Biography, The Andy Warhol Family Album, 2015, http://www.warhola.com/biography.html.

Chapter 6: Clone Yourself

1. Keith Ferrazzi and Tahl Raz, *Never Eat Alone: And Other Secrets to Success, One Relationship at a Time* (New York: Crown Business, 2014).

Chapter 7: Building Playbooks

1. Ray Dalio, *Principles: Life and Work* (New York: Simon & Schuster, 2017).

2. Nick Offerman as Richard "Dick" McDonald in *The Founder*, directed by John Lee Hancock (2016; New York, NY: FilmNation Entertainment).

3. Christopher Klein, "How McDonald's Beat Its Early Competition and Became an Icon of Fast Food," History.com, last modified August 7, 2019, https://www.history.com/news /how-mcdonalds-became-fast-food-giant.

4. Robert T. Kiyosaki and Sharon L. Lechter, *Rich Dad, Poor Dad: What the Rich Teach Their Kids About Money That the Poor and Middle Class Do Not!* (Paradise Valley, AZ: TechPress, 1998).

Chapter 8: Your Perfect Week

1. Ken Robinson and Lou Aronica, *Finding Your Element: How to Discover Your Talents and Passions and Transform Your Life* (New York: Viking, 2013).

2. Team Tony, "Stop Wasting Your Time!: Harness the Power of N.E.T. Time," Tony Robbins, March 6, 2020, https://www.tonyrobbins.com/productivity-performance/stop -wasting-your-time.

3. David Finkel, "New Study Shows You're Wasting 21.8 Hours a Week," *Inc.*, March 1, 2018, https://www.inc.com/david-finkel/new-study-shows-youre-wasting-218-hours-a-week.html.

Chapter 9: The Only 4 Time Hacks You Need

1. Trung T. Phan, "Pela Case, The $100m Sustainable Phone Case Startup That Created a Category," The Hustle, January 19, 2021, https://thehustle.co/01192021-pela-case.

Chapter 10: The "Test-First" Hiring Method

1. "The One Question I Ask in a Job Interview," GaryVee TV, YouTube, July 13, 2016, https://www.youtube.com/watch?v=kYPkCWREPy0.

Chapter 11: Transformational Leadership

1. Yaron Levi et al., "Decision Fatigue and Heuristic Analyst Forecasts" (prepublication manuscript, July 20, 2018), doi:10.31234/osf.io/mwv3q.

2. *Moneyball*, directed by Bennett Miller (Culver City, CA: Columbia Pictures, 2011).

Chapter 12: This "F-Word" Will Save Your Business

1. Shawn Baldwin, "The Great Resignation: Why Millions of Workers Are Quitting," CNBC, October 20, 2021, https://www.cnbc.com/2021/10/19/the-great-resignation-why -people-are-quitting-their-jobs.html.

2. Baldwin, "The Great Resignation."
3. Naina Dhingra et al., "Help Your Employees Find Purpose—or Watch Them Leave," McKinsey & Company, February 27, 2022, https://www.mckinsey.com/business-functions /people-and-organizational-performance/our-insights/help-your-employees-find-purpose -or-watch-them-leave.

Chapter 13: Dream BIG. Achieve Bigger

1. David Cameron Gikandi, *Happy Pocket Full of Money, Expanded Study Edition: Infinite Wealth and Abundance in the Here and Now* (Charlottesville, VA: Hampton Roads Publishing Company, 2015).
2. Primary-source interview; quotes from memory; name changed.
3. Brian Johnson, as quoted by Tim Ferriss on *The Tim Ferriss Show*.
4. Zat Rana, "Career Strategy: Don't Sell Sugar Water," CNBC, March 24, 2017, https://www.cnbc.com/2017/03/24/career-strategy-dont-sell-sugar-water.html.
5. The Strategic Coach Team, "10x Is Easier Than 2x," Strategic Coach, accessed May 9, 2022, https://resources.strategiccoach.com/the-multiplier-mindset-blog/10x-is-easier-than-2x.
6. Alyssa Hertel, "Where Is Michael Phelps Now? Olympics Legend Focused on Mental Health and Family," *USA Today*, July 22, 2021, https://www.usatoday.com/story/sports /olympics/2021/07/22/michael-phelps-olympics-swimming-where-is-he-now/7930625002.
7. Andy Bull, "Michael Phelps Taught a Lesson for Once—By Singapore's Joseph Schooling," *The Guardian*, August 13, 2016, https://www.theguardian.com/sport/2016/aug/13/michael -phelps-taught-a-lesson-for-once-by-singapores-joseph-schooling.
8. Gary Ng, "The Top 100 Meeting: Apple's Ultra Secretive Managerial Tool," *iPhone in Canada* (blog), May 7, 2011, https://www.iphoneincanada.ca/news/the-top-100-meeting -apples-ultra-secretive-managerial-tool.

Chapter 14: The Preloaded Year

1. "Evolution and History of the Department of Energy and the Office of Environmental Management," Department of Energy, https://www.energy.gov/sites/prod/files/2014/03 /f8/EM_Overview_History.pdf.
2. Edward Teller, "Scientists in War and Peace," *Bulletin of the Atomic Scientists* 1, no. 6 (1946): 10–12.
3. Meir Kay, "A Valuable Lesson for a Happier Life," May 4, 2016, https://www.youtube.com /watch?v=SqGRnlXplx0.
4. Primary source interview.

Conclusion: The Buyback Life

1. Bryan Borzykowski, "Can Retirement Kill You?" Worklife, BBC, August 13, 2013, https://www.bbc.com/worklife/article/20130813-the-dark-side-of-the-golden-years.

Index

Italicized page numbers indicate charts.